EFFECTIVE SMALL GROUP COMMUNICATION

James Gerber

Effective ✳
Small ✳
Group ✳
Communication

By **Ernest G. Bormann,** University of Minnesota
Nancy C. Bormann, Normandale State Junior College

 Burgess Publishing Company • Minneapolis

5 6 7 8 9 0

Preface

In many first courses in speech communication, the new emphasis on communication theory and practice, rather than on public speaking, highlights the importance of small group communication for today's student. Students quickly see the relevance of the material to their daily lives and demand the instructor's insight and counsel.

Teaching small group communication as a unit in a first course is an exciting but difficult task. The instructor who wishes to provide a grounding in basic theories and concepts of small group behavior, leadership, and decision-making, as these relate to communicating in small groups, finds that time is short. Group experience is essential to student learning so there is little time for lecturing in depth. Textbooks for the first course often slight small group communication. Textbooks in discussion and group methods are too lengthy and complex for the student in the first course. Monographs in sociology, psychology, and social psychology dealing with group dynamics are esoteric and require much interpretation to make them useful to the college freshman and sophomore.

This book provides a way for the teacher to bridge the gap between what the experts know about small group communication and what beginning students need to know. Moreover, the book provides the information in a way that frees class time for student exercises and projects.

Although brief, this introduction to small group communication is complete and self-contained. The student requires no additional instruction to understand and use the material. Thus it is useful in many situations in which small groups of students learn and work together in classes and activities. Students participating in small group learning situations in modular scheduling will profit from studying this book even if they get no further instruction in small group communication. Students active in organizations have found this material useful and to-the-point. The book in an earlier edition proved popular and useful for thousands of students in adult education short courses, seminars, and workshops in leadership, group participation, and management training.

The authors' combined experience in teaching students in junior colleges, colleges, and universities has indicated that many students come to the first course in speech communication having learned fairly well how to compete, but they are often ignorant of the techniques needed for *working with others* once they leave the classroom. This book was written to fill the need for a practical, valid, group process text for the student who is taking his first and often *last* course in speech communication.

The aim of the book is to provide the reader with an introduction to basic communication theory as it is applied to the dynamics of small groups. The book emphasizes the effective and practical application of the theoretical insights and concepts to the daily communication problems of the student in committees, conferences, and small work group meetings. When teaching small group process ourselves, we use small task-oriented groups within the class so that all the students are learning, through practical exercises, the validity of the theories stated in the book.

This book contains no potion to be taken quickly for magic results. This is not a training manual that a person can follow "by the numbers" which will assure that he will become some sort of senior scout, able to be firm, decisive, flexible, and sensitive to the needs of others. Rather, it is a tool to be used in beginning one's education about the fascinating and complex things that happen when three or more people gather to work on a common problem.

Minneapolis, Minnesota
July, 1971

Ernest G. Bormann
Nancy C. Bormann

Contents

I

Introduction

Communicating in Small Groups

The college student in today's highly organized urban society often finds himself communicating in small groups for several hours each day. We live in a time when group techniques are widely used to teach many different subjects. Instructors often put students in groups to work on assignments. More and more, teachers are encouraged to break classes into smaller groups for instruction by modular scheduling in high schools and by experimental and flexible programming in junior, community, and liberal arts colleges. Students often informally get up small groups to study for examinations or to prepare for classes.

Much of our recreational and social life is related to groups. Think through your last week. How many times did you take part in casual social conversations with other people? How often did you go with a group to a party, a concert, or a movie? Groups are often used to increase understanding of social give-and-take and make people more sensitive to one another. Some groups such as sensitivity and encounter sessions are designed to increase individual understanding of group process and personal potential. The groups set up to increase social awareness are similar to the therapy groups that help people with problems such as alcoholism, drug addiction, juvenile delinquency, and mental illness.

The student who has a job with a business, religious, or educational organization usually works with others in a small group. In addition, the working student takes part in business meetings, committee meetings, and conferences as part of his duties.

The committee session and business conference are really the core of any sound program of communication for an organization. The small task-oriented group meeting can tell people directly about important matters in a setting where *they can ask questions and make comments.* No form of written or pictorial communication can make this claim! In addition, the meetings of small groups can build a feeling of commitment and involvement, a sense of group and organization loyalty. The person who is part of any organization identifies more readily with a small team.

No matter what we do or where we live, in a highly developed country we will find ourselves spending much of our time in work groups. Basic to successful participation in these groups is our skill in and our understanding of small group communication. The focus of this book is upon productive participation in groups that are set up to do a job.

Part I

Objectives

After you have studied Part I you should be better able to:

* *evaluate a group.*

* *estimate a group's level of cohesiveness on the basis of the way the members communicate with one another.*

* *discover the role and status structure of a group from the communication patterns.*

* *describe a group's norms in both the task and social dimensions.*

* *compute the attraction of a group for individual members by estimating the rewards and costs of the group for each.*

* *design a program of action that you can take to improve the cohesiveness of a given group.*

* *respond quickly to situations that arise in a meeting in such a way that you help to build a positive social climate.*

The Dynamics of Good Groups

WE HAVE ALL WORKED WITH OTHERS before arriving at a careful, systematic study of group dynamics. Because of our previous experiences, then, we all have many ideas and beliefs about the way people work in committees which can be useful as starting places for the study of small group communication. In many ways, however, our "common sense" and vague ideas about how groups work can stand in the way of increased understanding and improved performance.

Part I contains definitions of key concepts based upon extensive study and systematic research into group process. Because we present the definitions in simple and straightforward terms, you should not conclude that we are simply restating the common sense meanings for the terms. Learn the precise definitions because they are crucial to your ability to analyze group process and to improve your participation in meetings.

Part I is devoted to the "good group" and answers such basic questions as: What is a task-oriented small group? How can I tell a good group when I see one? What makes groups tick? Why do people have personality conflicts in groups? How can I generate group loyalty? Why do groups have apathetic members?

Definition of a Work Group

A basic definition. The task-oriented small group is composed of three or more people working together to do a clearly specified job or to reach a common goal.

Two-person interview excluded. We do not deal with the dialogue or two-person interview because the introduction of a third person changes the nature of the working and social relationships.

Therapy groups excluded. We do not examine therapy groups, sensitivity training (T-groups), or encounter groups. These have as their primary purpose the improvement of the mental or social health of the individual by having him work out his personal problems through the group. Our aim is to concentrate on groups with a common problem to solve or a job to do.

Groups may be short term. Examples of short-term groups would be: A committee meeting for the PTA, a study group for the League of Women Voters, a business conference, a discussion group at a campus religious house, or a committee for a student government project.

Groups may be long term. Examples of long-term groups would be: A project team in a research and development section of a computer company, an ad hoc committee to study metropolitan problems, a student and faculty committee to study curriculum changes, standing committees of campus organizations, the basic on-the-job group where an individual earns a living, and the family.

The Proper Size for Good Groups

A good size for a group. Research in small groups indicates that five is an excellent number for a work group. Members of groups with fewer than five people complain that their groups are too small. Groups composed of an even number of people are not as efficient as groups totaling an odd number. Five or seven is a better size for a committee than four, six, or eight. Five is the dividing point. Larger groups change character and have different patterns of communication.

When groups grow larger. In groups of five or less, all participants speak to one another, even those who speak very little. In groups of seven or more, the quiet members cease to talk to one another and talk only to the top people — the leader or the high status persons. As groups get even larger, the talk centralizes more and more around a few people. Group interaction falls off. In groups of thirteen or more, a small group of from five to seven usually holds the discussion while the others simply watch and listen. In permanent work groups larger than thirteen, the tendency is to form small groups (cliques) within the larger group.

When forming a committe. If you can appoint the members to a committee or work group, be sure that you have an odd number and try to make it five or seven. If the group must be larger than seven, consider the use of subcommittees to do some of the projects.

When the work group is long term. If the permanent work group is larger than seven, watch for the formation of cliques within the larger group, and examine their development in the light of group process. These small groups can be mobilized for the good of the larger unit. The danger is that if they are disgruntled with the leadership of the larger group, they may fight its goals.

Groups Must Socialize As Well As Work

The work group is a social event. When several people share ideas or produce a product, a whole *social* dimension is added. The first question in the mind of every person in a new work group is: HOW DO I RELATE TO THESE OTHER PEOPLE AS A HUMAN BEING? Every member wants this question answered, and he wants it answered early! Moreover, even after he has been in the group for months or even years, he wants the answer repeated, however briefly, each day!

Do not ignore the social dimension of your work group. Talking about hobbies, reading habits, sports, travels, family, and friends is important to the social health of the group. If you are calling the first meeting for a new group, take a few minutes at the beginning for such talk.

(1) Have an informal "get acquainted period" scheduled during which refreshments are served. (More suitable for a committee or study group meeting in a home.)

(2) Or, begin the first meeting by having each participant talk about himself, his interests, how he feels about an important topic under consideration.

(3) Or, adjourn the first meeting a bit early and encourage people to stick around afterwards. People often relax and feel free to

say things when the meeting is over that they would not say during the first session. If it is a business meeting, you may ask the group to break for coffee in the cafeteria after the session.

If you are chairman of a continuing group, supervisor of an office force, or president of a campus organization, spend some time in each work session for similar talk.

One businessman in a communication seminar asked, "How can you justify wasting the company's time socializing on the job?" To which another executive answered, as we would have, "How can you afford not to?"

The importance of the social dimension. If a person feels that the others like, admire, and respect him, that they enjoy his company, and consider his ideas important, he can let his hair down and turn his full attention to doing the job. Such an atmosphere of trust and understanding should be the goal of every participant, and *particularly* of every manager, chairman, moderator, or leader of a work group. The group member is seldom sure about these matters, however, and as he goes about the job, talking about important problems and exchanging information, he may think that some work-related comment is a threat to his standing in the group, or to him as a person, or that it constitutes a slur on those he represents. He may feel that a comment suggesting that his committee has fallen down on the job, is really a criticism of him as a person rather than an evaluation of the source of a problem. Immediately, he is on guard, preoccupied with social matters rather than with task considerations.

How important is the social dimension? Consider two groups composed of the same sorts of people and doing the same job; one can be torn with dissention, absenteeism, and low productivity, while the other, comprised of members who like each other, may work harmoniously and effectively. What is the difference? For the most part you can say one has a healthy social dimension and the other has not.

Groups Must Work As Well As Socialize

The work group is a task event. We are only discussing those groups that have a job to do. Inevitably the members will expect to, and usually want to, concentrate on the job. If the group is meeting for a discussion or conference, they will want to get to the agenda and start talking about it. If the group is a message-processing unit, the members will want to start reading the mail, absorbing the memorandums, filing important papers, drafting letters, holding conferences, and so forth. If it is a political action group, the members will want to lay plans and get organized.

Working with others is more difficult than working alone. We usually enjoy having company while we work, but coordinating effort is difficult. Handling ideas in a group meeting is not a simple task. Working with several people to achieve a common goal complicates matters. Do not expect a group to work with the same concentration and efficiency as one good individual working alone. Groups require structure and coordination. Coordination takes efficient planning and communication. The group's ability to concentrate its talents and energy on the task, its ability to mobilize its resources, will be hampered by poor plans, misunderstandings, faulty reasoning, inadequate concepts, bad information, and, most importantly, by the way directions and orders are given and received. *A whole book could be devoted to the subject of giving and receiving orders.* Orders must be given but, when you give another person an order, the task and social areas come into conflict. If the group member thinks the direction is an indication that the leader feels superior to him or that he is using the group for his own purposes, the order may be misunderstood or not obeyed even though it is a good one.

Evaluating the Work Group

Evaluate the social health. A good work group has high morale. The members are happy with the group, they enjoy working with the others on the job, and are pleased with their place in the group. They receive a sense of belonging and a feeling of personal satisfaction from their role.

Evaluate the productivity. A good group gets things done. It reaches its goals with a minimum of wasted motion. It turns out a large quantity of high quality work, wins games, solves problems, makes good decisions.

Balance both the social health and the productivity. Some people think that productivity is all that counts. But the individual should gain a sense of satisfaction and worth from his participation in the group. We do not believe that the individual exists solely for the group. The group has certain duties and responsibilities to the individual.

Cohesiveness, the Key to Successful Work Groups

Cohesiveness defined. Cohesiveness refers to the ability of the group to stick together. Another term for the same quality is *group loyalty.* A highly cohesive group is one in which the members work for the good of the group. They are tightly knit, and they help one another. They exhibit team spirit. They reflect the motto of Alexander Dumas' *Three Musketeers,* "All for one and one for all."

Cohesiveness encourages productivity, morale, and communication. Groups with high group loyalty have greater productivity, higher morale, and better communication than groups with little cohesiveness.

(1) Cohesive production groups do more work because members take the *initiative* and help one another. They distribute the work load among themselves. They take up the slack in times of stress. Workers in groups with little cohesiveness tend to stand around and wait for assignments from their supervisors. They do only what they are told to do and no more. They do not care about the work of the others. While members of cohesive groups volunteer to help one another, people in groups with little cohesiveness "keep their noses clean" and "look out for number one."

(2) The morale of the members is closely tied to the cohesiveness. If the group is important to them, people pay attention to its problems. They spend time and effort in behalf of the group, and they glory in its successes.

(3) The more cohesive the group, the more efficient the communication within the group. We will have much more to say about this when we discuss small group communication in Part III. Here we will simply note that cohesiveness encourages disagreements and questions. Both are necessary to communication. Members of highly cohesive groups disagree among themselves. They cannot stand by and watch the

others do a shoddy job or make a wrong decision. Their group is at stake. They must speak up and do what they can to assure its success. Such disagreements improve the quality and quantity of the work by assuring a high level of communication. Cohesiveness encourages questions. In the cohesive group, every member knows his place and is secure. His position is not threatened if he admits that he does not know something. Indeed, the welfare of the group requires that each member have adequate information. The group rewards questions that help it achieve its goals. Likewise, the important member does not feel insulted when people pin him down and ask for more information. He is more interested in the welfare of the group than in his own personal feelings. Since the group largely succeeds or fails depending upon the efficiency of its communication, the cohesive group encourages its members to work cooperatively to come to a meeting of the minds.

The symptoms of low cohesiveness. Groups with little cohesiveness have meetings which are quiet, polite, boring, and apathetic. The general attitude of the members is reflected by their tense posture, their sighs and yawns. Their attitude is, "Let's get this meeting over with. I am uncomfortable." People seldom disagree; there is little give-and-take discussion. Often a question is followed by a long pause. Even important decisions are handled quickly, with little comment.

The symptoms of high cohesiveness. Work meetings of highly cohesive groups tend to be noisy, full of joshing, personal byplay, disagreement, and even argument. They often run overtime and people may continue the discussion after the meeting is over. Few important questions are raised without a thorough airing.

Group Process

Research in small groups. We are now going to come to the heart of the matter: what makes the group tick. What follows is not going to be simple, but it is absolutely essential for an understanding of work groups. Group process is complex — not difficult, but complex. The difference between our approach now and the helpful hints treatment of conference leadership is that we will explain some of the results of the most recent basic research in group process. Sociologists and psychologists did not discover work groups until relatively recently. A. Paul Hare collected a list of studies in small groups from 1890 to 1958 and found that from 1890 to 1899, there was about one study published every two years. Nowadays hundreds of research studies in small groups are published every year.

Why so much interest in basic research in groups? The second World War was a turning point. The war put a premium on productivity and morale in business, industry, and the armed services. We had to produce. Millions of dollars were spent by government and industry to study the factors that go into productivity. The dynamic factors within a small group proved extremely important to both concerns.

The test tube group. One of the important techniques used to study group process was the test tube group. The studies in group process, communication, and leadership at the University of Minnesota have used this approach. The test tube groups are composed of strangers and are set up under carefully controlled conditions. The groups have no formal structure. Every member is a peer – that is, they are all equals. They do have a clear job and a specific time limit. In the test tube groups, the normal operations of a work group are speeded up by "pressure cooker" methods. The basic patterns of group process take place quickly and without distracting variables so they may be discovered and charted.

Role specialization is inevitable. The first important discovery is that after several hours, the members of the test tube groups begin to specialize, and some members come to be looked up to and some are looked down on by the others. *We have never observed a group in our studies at Minnesota where this did not happen, and no such group has been reported by other investigators.*

When it becomes clear to a person that he is specializing and when the group discovers that he is doing so, he takes a *place* in the group. He has his particular *role* in this particular group. It is the part he expects to play and the part the others expect him to play. It is indeed comparable to the concept of roles in plays, and one interesting finding of the research is that individuals change "personality" as they go from group to group. The coed who has such a sparkling personality in class and enjoys kidding around with the fellows may be quiet, devout, and reserved in her church circle. She may be ill-tempered and bossy with her family. Think of yourself. In one group you may be a take-charge person who gets things rolling. In another you are likable, joshing, and fun-loving, but not a leader at all. In a third group you are a quiet, steady, and responsible worker. Not so? Think of your first group as your own family. Your second, the people with whom you usually eat lunch. The third, you at your dorm, fraternity, sorority, or in class. Now, which is the real you? That isn't even a sensible question, really, because you change roles from group to group, and your personality is to some extent determined by the people around you. *The basic principle is: a member's role is worked out jointly by the person and the group.*

For this reason, also, you should not blame the group's problems on innate unchangeable personality traits inherent in a troublesome person. Groups can be more neurotic than individuals, and they love to blame their troubles on one member — make him the scapegoat for their failures. If you understand the nature of roles and group process, you no longer will make that mistake. Instead of wishing you could get rid of Bill so you could have a decent outfit, you ask what the group is doing to Bill to make him act as he does. You begin to look for ways to change the role structure of the work group so every member can live up to his potential. You begin to utilize the entire resources of the group.

Status. Once everyone has found his place, a second important thing happens. The group judges the relative worth of each role. They give the roles they judge more valuable a higher status than the others. After a group has been working together for several hours, a trained observer can arrange the status ladder by watching the way the members talk and act. They will talk directly and more often to the people they consider important. High status people talk more to the entire group. The high status people receive more consideration from the others. The others listen to what a high status individual says; they often stop what they are doing to come to him; they stop talking to hear him, and they agree more and more emphatically with him. The group tends to ignore and cut off comments by low status members.

Struggle for status. Since much esteem and prestige reward goes to the "leader" and other high status members, several members compete for the top positions. In this competition they come into conflict; there are disagreements. The group's energy is directed to the question of who will win out and attention is drawn away from the work. In extreme cases the struggles become heated, and the group gets bogged down. Every new group must go through a "shakedown cruise" during which they test roles and find out who is "top dog," who is best liked, and so forth. During the "shakedown cruise," secondary tensions mount, and people who are contending for leadership come into conflict.

The basic process. How do roles emerge? How does specialization and status come about? Here is the intriguing core of what makes small groups tick. Here our research has been thorough and very fascinating. Perhaps the process of role emergence could best be explained through the use of a model. Just as physicians learn that individual anatomy varies, so work groups will vary in each instance. Physicians, nonetheless, begin their study of anatomy in a textbook, and this, basically, is the way group roles emerge:

Five students are placed in a test-tube group. They have not been given any role assignment; that is, no one has said that Joe will be secretary and Bill, leader. They do not know one another, and they have no reason to view any of the others as anything but equals. As a group, they do have a clear goal and a definite set of jobs that have to be done. In addition to Joe and Bill, the group contains Harry, Don, and Wilbur.

We could just as well have used an all-female group for our example because the dynamics would be the same as for an all-male group. When we have groups composed of men and women, however, several additional factors serve to complicate matters.

Sexual attractions among men and women will change the social dynamics of a group. Leadership is also complicated by the sex factor. Men tend to resist the leadership of a woman, no matter how capable, and will malinger or actively work against her efforts to structure the group's work. In recent years with the rise of Women's Liberation we have noticed a similar attitude on the part of some women. We have made several case studies in which two or more women members of a group have refused to follow any plans suggested by a man as a matter of principle. We have also noticed a greater willingness on the part of some men to allow a woman to lead a group, apparently as a result of recent concern for woman's place in society. When a group becomes a battleground for conflict between the sexes, the possibility of successful group work is slim.

To keep our description of the process as basic as possible, therefore, we will use a same sex, in this case an all-male group, for our purposes.

Each of the men in our model group could do every task that is required to have the group succeed. Each, however, can do some of the things the group needs to have done better than others. Joe, for example, has been trained in technical mechanical matters. He is talented in planning and building machines. Bill is more adept at making plans for group action. He likes to divide a job into its component parts and find people to do the various tasks. Harry is good at testing ideas. The group has many different specific tasks that must be done, and to do them, they have to depend upon the resources and skills of the five members.

Remember that the work group is a social event. In addition to getting the job done, the group needs to take care of certain housekeeping chores of a social sort. Again all five could do all of the social things, but each is more skilled at some than at others.

We will begin the process of group structuring with a social concern. The members feel the typical primary tension common to the first group meeting. Don and Wilbur have been tension releasers in other groups and both have some talent in this human relations skill. They both enjoy the rewards that come from releasing social tension—the laughter, the social approval, being well liked. Generally, the person who assumes the tension release function becomes the most popular member. Don and Wilbur are both alert to any signs of primary tension, and they find a stiff social atmosphere uncomfortable. They both must try to "break the ice." Don has his characteristic way of being funny. He begins by making small talk about anything that comes into his head. When he sees someone respond in a friendly way, he makes a mildly insulting comment and laughs to indicate it is all in fun. In addition, he has memorized a vast store of "stories" which he tells at the slightest provocation.

Wilbur also has his own style of humor. He is something of a clown and pantomimist. He is clever at doing impersonations and has an expressive face. Don begins to break the ice by making small talk and then insulting Harry. He waits for the response. He does not get a big laugh. The others may smile a bit, but their response is tentative. Don cannot tell whether they liked his sally or not. Wilbur is encouraged to give it a try, and he does a little pantomime routine.

He watches to see how the others liked his little act. Again the response is half-hearted. Don tries again; Wilbur takes another turn. The others watch the two demonstrate their wares, and gradually they make up their minds as to whether Don or Wilbur should specialize in releasing tension or whether they might share the function. In the latter case, they would be affectionately referred to as a "couple of clowns."

The selection process is accomplished subconsciously. The group members are generally not aware of what is going on. They notice only that, say, Don is tactless and something of a smart aleck and that Wilbur is really pretty funny. When Harry comes to this conclusion, he begins to laugh at Wilbur and to ignore Don's attempts at humor. Then Bill and Joe may begin to see Wilbur's humor and begin to laugh at him. If Don continues to insult people or tell his "old" stories, the others may begin to groan and in other ways let him know that he ought to "knock it off." After a time, Wilbur will do more and more of the tension releasing and Don will stop and move on to other functions. At this point, the struggle for the high status function of being well liked and releasing social tensions will be over. Wilbur will be a specialist. He will expect to be funny, and the group will expect him to step in when things get tense and inject a little humor to relax the atmosphere. If Wilbur fails to play his role—if he appears at a group meeting one day with a long face and is quiet and glum, the group will resent his change. Wilbur, they'll say, is not himself today. They'll ask him if he's sick. Should Wilbur try to get serious and make an important decision for the group, they will probably laugh at him.

Once the social tensions are broken, the group will go to work. Now they need someone with a "take charge" skill to step in and get them rolling. Bill and Harry have done this task for other groups, and they enjoy the rewards of being the take charge person. As soon as Harry feels that the primary tension has been released, he grows restless and wants to get down to business. He says, "All right. Let's get going. I suggest we begin by . . ." He does not get immediate obedience. The other members do not say, "That's a good idea. Let's go." They seldom even nod approval. They say little one way or another. Now Bill is encouraged to try his hand. He says, "I don't quite understand what you mean. Would you run through that again?" Harry patiently explains his plan of action, thinking to himself that Bill is not very bright. Bill now sees what Harry is driving at but says, "I'm not sure that we have to do it that way. How about this? Wouldn't this be better?" Bill now makes a suggestion of his own as to how the group might go about its work. Gradually the group begins to follow Bill's directions and orders more often than they follow Harry's. At that point, Bill will have emerged as the group's *leader*.

In much the same way, each person gradually learns that he is to specialize in certain social and task concerns. Each is led to specialize by the group's encouragement. They agree with him when he does what they want him to do, and they disagree when he does not and thus discourage him from a role they do not feel they need or will not accept him in.

A given person does not have a complete monopoly on the role functions he "ends up with," but he will carry out most of these assigned functions for the group. That is, Harry may turn out to have a wry wit which the group appreciates because it is intellectual and subtle compared to Wilbur's more physical and obvious humor, so Harry is indeed witty from time to time even though Wilbur does most of the tension releasing. In the same way, Joe may take charge of getting certain technical jobs completed even though Bill is the member who does this for the group most of the time. Although some roles are established quickly and easily, the role of *leader* is among the last to emerge. Sometimes no leader emerges at all. At Minnesota, John Geier made a careful in-depth study of sixteen such groups working together for as long as twelve weeks. Almost one-third never succeeded in having a leader emerge or in having the other roles settle down. The groups in which a leader failed to emerge were uniformly unsuccessful at their job and were, furthermore, socially punishing to their members. They were torn with strife, they wasted much time, and they frustrated the people in them. Much of their energy went into contention for high status positions, and little was left over for productive effort. These groups suffered from absenteeism and low levels of cohesiveness.

Those groups in which a leader emerged and the roles settled down in such a pattern that every member was happy with his place were successful. Members of such groups knew what to expect when they came to work. They knew what they were supposed to do and how the other members of the group would react to them. They could relax and "be themselves." Typically, the test tube groups experienced a dramatic increase in cohesiveness when the role structure became stable.

Norms. During the "shakedown cruise" as the group is developing specialized roles for its members, another process is at work creating common ways of doing things. We call these common or standard operating procedures *group norms.* Groups develop norms dealing with both the task dimension and the social interactions. Groups with clear goals will try to achieve them and, because of the response they get from other groups and organizations, they soon learn whether their work norms are successful or unsuccessful. The basketball team whose goal is to win games learns soon enough how good it is at its task. Another set of norms governs the way the members get along with one another as people. The members may adopt a common way of dressing or of wearing their hair or of talking with one another. They may even develop an unusual vocabulary when meeting as a group. Social norms are less obviously tied to achieving group goals and thus often become more unusual and bizarre than the norms related to the task.

(1) *Aping behavior.* One of the most important features of group dynamics is the power of nonverbal and verbal suggestion to get people to act as others around them are acting. "Follow-the-leader" impulses are so instinctive that we call them aping behavior because apes and monkeys often mimic the things they see other apes, monkeys, or people do.

A person stops on the street and begins to look at the sky. Soon several other people stop and look upward. When a knot of people are standing, peering towards the heavens, the impulse of someone coming upon the group to stop and do likewise is strong.

Suppose a group of students are meeting for the first time. A member confidently slouches back in his seat and puts his feet on the table. He makes an informal and slangy comment about the class and the purpose of the meeting. Another member tips his chair back against the blackboard and agrees with the first, using the same sort of language. Several more members follow suit and soon the pressure on the one or two remaining people in the group to also assume an informal posture and use slangy speech is very strong. The group develops an informal way of gesturing and uses slangy, inside-dopester, language in its discussions.

(2) *The pressure to conform and cohesiveness.* As the group develops higher levels of cohesiveness the pressure on group members to adopt the group's norms increases. The more attractive the group, the more likely the member will be to do as the group does even though its norms are in conflict with those of other groups to which he belongs. Many times parents of teen-agers discover that their norms for attractive clothing or hair styles are in conflict with those of a highly cohesive peer group, and they often lose in their attempts to influence their children's dress and hair style.

(3) *Overt pressure for conformity.* Members of highly cohesive groups are sensitive to failure to act as the group norms require because they often see such failure as evidence of lack of commitment to the group. They often put overt pressure on deviant members to achieve conformity to group norms. Members who see nonconformity as a threat to the group usually take steps to bring the nonconformist into line. Often they begin by talking to the member. The first comments are usually light and humorous. If the group norm is to wear dirty and obviously patched blue jeans, the members may begin to make cracks about the well-dressed member. The criticism is thus sweetened by a laugh and the release of tension that it produces.

If gentle teasing and humorous comments do not change the behavior, the communication may become more cutting and may contain ridicule and satire. Instead of laughing with the nonconformist, they now begin to laugh at him. If the member still does not conform, the others will often change from satire and ridicule to direct and serious persuasion. If the deviant member still remains a nonconformist, the others may reject him and isolate him from future communications.

(4) *Changing group norms.* The norms of a group are something like the habits of an individual. The norms may develop haphazardly, and some may be useful and productive for

both task efficiency and member satisfaction. Others may be inefficient and punishing to members. Like habits, norms can be changed by accident or by plan. Groups can discuss their norms, discover their weaknesses, and by conscious effort change them.

In one student group composed of three men and two women, the coeds became very bored and unproductive members. When the group paused and viewed a video tape of one of their meetings and discussed the problem, they discovered that the men had developed the habit of not paying any attention to the substantive comments of the women. The men listened and responded when the coeds made social comments, but when the group got down to the task they ignored the ideas of the women. As a result of the discussion of the group's do-not-listen-to-the-women norm, the men resolved to listen in the future. When they fell back into the old habits, the women reminded them of their resolve. Gradually a new and more productive norm developed, and the coeds became interested and productive members of the group.

Building Cohesive Groups

Cohesiveness is dynamic. To build cohesiveness for your group you need to know some of the dynamics of group process. Every member of the work group is constantly experiencing pushes into and pulls away from the group. The cohesiveness of the group fluctuates from day to day. It is one of the dynamic changing features of groups. A unit that is highly cohesive this year – an effective, hard-hitting group – may suffer a series of reverses, change members, and lose cohesiveness so that next year it is in serious trouble.

The work group is under constant external pressures. Some of these pressures aid cohesiveness and some detract from it. If the group comes in competition with similar groups, cohesiveness is usually increased. One reason athletic teams develop such high levels of team spirit and will-to-win is that they compete with other teams in a win-or-lose situation. Coaches know the importance of cohesiveness and how to build it. On the other hand, a *competing* group may put pressure on a member to lure him away from a group and thus decrease his feeling of commitment. If you wish to examine the cohesiveness of your group, you must look to the other groups that are competing for the loyalty of the members. This is to say, the attractiveness of his group for a given person is partly dependent on the *next best group* that he could join. This becomes the comparison group. If the next best group becomes more attractive, the person may leave his present group (job) for the other group (another organization).

Make your group rewarding. If you want to know how attractive your group is to a person, total up the rewards it furnishes him, subtract the costs, and the remainder is an index of group attractiveness. A typical dictionary definition of *reward* is that it is a "recompense" that is given "for some service or attainment." A *cost* is the opposite of a reward. Rewards furnished each member by the group build cohesiveness; costs extracted from him discourage group loyalty and, if they grow too heavy, he will leave the group.

Individual motivation. To understand how a group can reward a person, we must first understand human needs and wants in general. Professor William S. Howell of the University of Minnesota, a leading authority on persuasion, points out that motives are "sources of energy" within the individual that move (motivate) him to "pursue selected alternates." Each person has a set of motives that give him the energy to move from his bed in the morning and pursue his daily activities. He could pursue a number of alternatives, but he selects the path that leads him to work with a particular group. Why one group rather than another? The answer depends upon his motivation.

Do not confuse *motivate* with *persuade.* You do not wire people with motives; they already have motives. People do things for their reasons, not yours, and you must plug into the energy already there. To persuade people, you must provide them with rewards that they find attractive because of their present needs.

Although people have very different motive structures, progress has been made in recent years toward a sensible general description of what makes people tick. Our brief outline is based on the explanations of such social scientists as A. H. Maslow and G. W. Allport and Howell's adaptation of their work.

The key to this explanation of human motivation is the *sequential* arrangement of basic needs. Some needs take priority over others, and these more basic needs must be satisfied first. Only when the lower needs are satisfied can higher level needs emerge. Picturing the motives as rungs on a ladder helps visualize the priorities:

Figure 1 illustrates the deficit ladder of human motivations. These motives are basic universals common to everyone, and they can be thought of as minimum essentials. A lack at any level is usually sufficient to trigger a person's energy resources and make him seek out rewards that will satisfy the need.

(1) *Physiological needs.* The first and most important rung of the ladder consists of the physiological needs — the most elementary and universal. These include such things as food, drink, activity, sleep, and sex. A thirsty man thinks of little else but drink. When he has all the water he can drink, however, other needs come to the surface. He begins to climb the ladder. The basic principle is that *unsatisfied needs are motivators of behavior.* When basic needs are satisfied and the first rung is reached, the unsatisfied needs of the next rung begin to dominate the individual's attention and actions.

(2) *Security needs.* We want to be secure — to have a predictable and organized life. We want to look into the future and know pretty well what will happen.

(3) *Social needs.* When the need for security is largely filled, the social needs begin to dominate. These are extremely important in developing a cohesive work group because they are the needs the group is uniquely equipped to gratify. They include the need to belong to a group and to give and receive acceptance.

(4) *Status and esteem needs.* When the social needs are satisfied, the desire for status and esteem becomes dominant. We need

to feel that we stand high in the eyes of others. We want a good reputation and position. We need prestige. Associated with the need for prestige is the desire for esteem. There are two sides to this motive — a public and a private side. The public side is that we need to be highly regarded by others. We need recognition, respect, and appreciation. This is not the same as status. For example, we gain status because of our reputation or because we inherited wealth, no matter what kind of person we are. Esteem is earned by our association with others. The private side is that we need to like ourselves. We want to feel self-confident, to have a good image of ourselves, and to feel that we really are important. Members of affluent societies often find their physiological and security needs largely satisfied, but they seldom have all of the status and esteem they want. Most of us are struggling to climb the upper rungs of the deficit ladder. Here is where work groups can provide some of their most powerful rewards.

(5) *Unselfishness.* The deficit ladder includes only the selfish motives — needs closely related to preserving our individual self and gratifying our ego. We look to these motives when we are out for "number one." We must always remember, however, that people often act unselfishly. They go out of their way to help others; they deny their own status to raise the status of others; they make personal sacrifices for the good of the group.

(6) *The desire to work.* The deficit ladder does not account for the drive to work. The notion that individuals are essentially mean, lazy, slothful, and want only to avoid work is a holdover from an old theological view of man. Recent social science and medical research indicates that we need and seek out work. The drive for workmanship is so strong that if it is frustrated on the day-to-day job, the individual will develop hobbies that give it release. He will have a home workshop, remodel his house, or landscape his yard. Psychiatrist Karl Menninger judges that "we must work in order to live . . ." Indeed, occupational therapy — giving the patient work that he can do — is an integral part of psychiatric treatment.

People do not have to be coerced, goaded, and forced to work for a group. They will seek out opportunities to do worthwhile and satisfying labor. An influential contemporary expert on management, Douglas McGregor, advocates *achievement* reward as the key to modern management.

Group rewards. Groups can furnish rewards at each rung of the deficit ladder. Insofar as your group furnishes you with more rewards more abundantly than the next best group you could join, you will find it attractive and you will work for the group.

(1) *Material rewards.* The work group may give a member material rewards. It may give him a salary, bonuses, or other cash benefits. Money can satisfy a number of motives; certainly it buys the things that fulfill the basic physiological needs, food, drink, shelter, and health care.

The group may also give a member indirect material benefits. Other members may help him make business contacts. Becoming a member of the country club may increase an insurance broker's sales.

However, just as the group may satisfy basic physiological needs, it may frustrate them. A member may make less money by staying with a particular group. He may receive fewer fringe benefits, sell less insurance, or even lose business because of his association. When this happens, the group's attraction is weakened.

The pull of cold cash offered by a given group is a function of the next best offer. If his present group pays him $8,000 per year and the next best job has a salary of $5,000, a member will find his present group much more attractive than if the next best offer is $7,500. Of course, if the offer is $9,000, the present group will begin to cost him. He may remain with his present group because it gives him other rewards, but he will not be as strongly drawn as he was when the group was giving him superior monetary rewards.

When a leader seeks to hire a man from another group, he often thinks first of offering more material rewards to appeal to the man's physiological needs. He suggests an increase in salary, greater fringe benefits, and perhaps more money in the future.

The leader of a group may use money to encourage greater effort in behalf of the group. He may give salary increases or bonuses as incentives for meeting individual quotas or for doing an outstanding job. The physiological needs are basic and appeals to them are effective; their continued use testifies to that.

However, when the basic physiological needs are met, a person no longer works for them. More money at this stage will do little to make a man work harder or be more loyal to the group. Douglas McGregor makes the point strongly in his new approach to management; he suggests that money may be a dissatisfier in that a man who feels he deserves more (is worth more) than he gets will be dissatisfied. In this case, money does not serve as a reward to greater effort.

Money is an obvious reward, but it is mentioned here only to lay the groundwork for the less obvious ones.

(2) *Security rewards.* The group can provide its members with security. Money, of course, can also purchase insurance policies, mutual funds, and retirement annuities to give security. In addition, if the group has established ways of meeting and working, it provides the individual with a secure social environment. He knows what to expect when he works with other members of the group, and he finds such security rewarding.

(3) *Social rewards.* The group can provide its members with powerful social rewards. It can make a person feel that he belongs. Our psychiatrists, novelists, and playwrights continually emphasize the role of loneliness in mental disturbances. A work group can provide an individual with contacts with other people who know him as a person and like and respect him. In one of the groups studied at the University of Minnesota, where classes can be very large and commuting students absorbed in their own busy lives, a foreign student said that, for the first time in his two years in this country, he had gotten to know some American students and to make some real friends. He found this fully as important to him as the work satisfactions and material rewards he received.

On the other hand, the group can be socially punishing.

The social relations may be in a constant flux. The individual never knows for sure what is expected of him. He may feel rejected and the group may treat him as a person of little worth. When this happens, he may leave the group.

(4) *Prestige rewards.* The work group can provide its members with prestige rewards. When a group develops a good reputation, it sheds its prestige on all the members, thus increasing a person's reputation in the community. The individual will boast of his membership in an elite organization. He may even wear some public sign of his membership, such as a pin, a ring, or a special piece of clothing.

Conversely, the group may have a bad reputation, perhaps from having unsavory characters as members or from an extended string of failures. The high school gang with members who have a police record or the ball team that is the conference doormat—these groups award their members little prestige.

Groups have a spongelike ability to absorb the prestige of their members. The group's reputation is enhanced when important people join. Voluntary organizations quite often print the names of famous and prestigious members on a letterhead. Work groups also develop a reputation in their own right. They gain prestige by doing a good job. Among production units, the one with the highest output of quality goods is the "best."

However, the prestige of a group is seldom constant. The group's efficiency depends on its cohesiveness, which tends to fluctuate in cycles. Cohesiveness grows and yields greater productivity which increases the prestige of the group which increases the cohesiveness which results in still greater task efficiency. Should this upward spiral be broken, the downward slide can begin. A change in personnel, a failure of some size, a loss of prestige (the public often likes to see the top dog stumble) will drop cohesiveness, which will further impair task efficiency, and the downward spiral begins. Good groups must always be on guard to keep overconfidence and complacency from starting the downward cycle.

(5) *Esteem rewards.* The group can provide its members with esteem rewards. If an individual becomes important within

the group—if he emerges as a leader, is well-respected, well liked, looked up to—he will receive esteem rewards. Time and time again a person who is given prestigeful work within the group, who does a good job, and who is recognized as an important and worthwhile worker, becomes more strongly drawn to his unit.

The work group may also deprive a person of his esteem needs. If the others make it clear to him that he is unimportant to them, they deprive him of his esteem needs. He will need a great deal of money or other reward to make up for such deprivation. Much of the nonparticipation, the so-called "dead wood" in organizations and work groups, results from this factor. Highly cohesive groups make every person feel that he is important to the team, a worthy individual doing his share—even though he does not speak up or do other than routine chores. The others, *at the very least,* assure him that they esteem him as a person and a fellow worker.

(6) *Work rewards.* The group can provide its members with work rewards, work satisfactions. The group can satisfy the instinct for workmanship in two ways. First, it may provide a person with an opportunity to do the kind of work he likes to do. A person's vocational choice is closely tied to his ultimate happiness and satisfaction. Some groups will provide an individual with the chance to do exciting and significant things. He may sacrifice some monetary rewards and prestige and esteem satisfactions if he is doing the job he loves to do. Second, the group provides him with other people who can appreciate a good job. Even when we know that we have done an excellent piece of work, we do not get maximum satisfaction until other people, whose opinion we respect, honestly and sincerely appreciate the job.

These work and esteem needs are often met in leadership positions. At the very time when the people working at menial jobs, jobs that provide few if any of these satisfactions, are demanding shorter hours, the managers work long hours above and beyond what is required. The higher the level of leadership, the greater the effort. The increase in commitment and dedication on the part of leaders in all kinds of groups is a function of the increased work and esteem satisfactions.

The work group can deprive its members of work satisfactions, also. The worker may be required to do tasks he finds dull or unchallenging. The family may require the mother to wash diapers, wipe runny noses, and scrub floors. If she finds such work unrewarding and unappreciated, she will find it distasteful to do or she may fail to do it at all. The highly cohesive groups studied at the University of Minnesota all developed ways in which the entire group (not just the leader) made it clear to a person that they appreciated the work he had done when he did a particularly good job. Even if someone enjoys his work and feels he is doing it well, he will become disgruntled if no one notices his efforts. As we said, people are not inherently lazy, but we do have to feel that what we are doing is important and, further, that what we are doing is appreciated.

(7) *Losing the self in a cause.* Some special groups generate cohesiveness by working for a good cause. Groups dedicated to religious and spiritual objectives or to causes may become highly cohesive. Many of today's liberation movements, such as the Black, Chicano, and Indian movements, provide people with the chance to work for a cause. Political and social revolutionary organizations, such as the Students for a Democratic Society, Women's Liberation, and Gay Liberation, also provide their members with the rewards that come from working for a cause.

Such groups provide an opportunity for the individual to transcend the self and find a larger meaning in life. The person who joins an organization and fights for a cause he believes in is taking positive action. He feels he is having an effect on his community and his country. Rewards of this type can create a level of commitment that exceeds any that result from appeals to the selfish motives on the deficit ladder. History is filled with examples of individuals who chose to give their lives fighting for a cause. People who feel they have a responsibility to make the world a better place often feel guilty if they do not take action. A group dedicated to a cause can assuage these guilt feelings. The group should spell out clearly its basic beliefs and reiterate them for all new members. Frequent statements of the group's purpose, clearly and forcibly put, will assure that everyone understands the common goals.

Group attraction for the individual. At any given moment, an individual feels the pull of his group because it satisfies one or more of his basic needs. He is pushed from the organization if he finds that one or more of these needs will never be met. In addition, his loyalty is determined by the *relative deprivation* he feels at each rung of the ladder. The man with inherited wealth may keep a low-paying professorship at a small college because he enjoys his job, while a poor man would move to a better-paying school. Likewise, if one group fails to satisfy a person's need for esteem, but he has other ways to gain these rewards from groups such as the family, church, or Boy Scouts, he may still remain loyal to this group because it enables him to meet his need for workmanship or fighting for a cause.

Clearly, if you understand the way a group can satisfy the motivations of its members, you are well on the way to understanding the *process* by which cohesiveness is generated within the group. The group member or leader who understands this process can really apply the advice that he should build the most highly cohesive group possible.

Group interaction builds cohesion. To this point we have been examining cohesiveness in terms of the total group attractiveness to each individual member. As all of the members interact during their meetings, they also generate powerful forces for cohesion.

(1) *Group fantasy chains.* One important way in which groups develop common ground among the members is by joking and talking about things that do not always have to do with the business at hand. If we watch a group that is working along quite well, they sometimes come to a point where they stumble and seem to lose the thread of the discussion. They are unable to get back on the track. The members slump down in their chairs, begin to fiddle with their papers or pencils, look bored. The talk dribbles off, and there are long pauses.

Then one member says something completely off the subject about some person who is not part of the meeting or about somebody he has read about or seen on TV or about something that has happened to him recently or about something he wishes would happen to him in the future. Another member responds with a laugh and adds onto the story. Another member joins in and soon the entire group comes alive. They all begin talking, and they grow emotional. They may laugh or express fear or sadness. Then, as abruptly as it started, the episode is broken off by someone who usually pulls the group back to work.

We call these moments of dramatization which excite the group members and in which all or most of them participate *group fantasy chains*. You should not get the impression we are using the term *fantasy* in the sense that the communication is like science fiction or like a fairy story. A group fantasy may deal with real-life situations and people. We mean by fantasy that the situtation is removed from the here-and-now reality of the group, and the people in the episode are not acting in the presence of the group members at this particular time.

The group fantasy chain works something like the dreams that we have as individuals. When we daydream about people we admire doing things we would like to do or when we see ourselves acting out things we would like to do, we reveal our values, our goals, and our motives. If someone knows our most intimate daydreams, he can tell a good deal about how we will act.

Group fantasy chains serve to create common dreams for a group of people and thus build common ground for future decisions. For example, suppose we set up a group of five college students and give them a task to do for a class. The students start to work and soon discover some difference of opinion as to how they should go about their job. They also discover that one member is very task-oriented and wants things to be carefully organized and another is rather carefree and keeps suggesting that the group make sure that no member has to spend too much time in the library. The talk begins to die out. Somebody mentions an upcoming social event on campus. There is a pause and the task-oriented member tries to bring the group back to the job at hand. The carefree member says in a joking way. "Oh, you're just like my father." Another member picks it up. "Really, what do you mean?" "My father is always driving us to get work done around the house. You can't take off a minute, and he comes around with a hammer or a paint brush or something." The group members begin to chime in with responses to an authority figure who is a taskmaster and with other examples of their own relating to similar characters and similar events.

In the course of chaining out the fantasy, they build a common ground about the style of leadership they prefer and their attitudes towards working for the group. Should the general attitude developed in the fantasy chain be negative towards authority figures who are constantly driving people to work, the taskmaster will undoubtedly not emerge as the leader of this particular group.

When groups chain out a number of fantasies of this sort over a period of time, they build a group culture, and they often allude to the heroes and villains of their fantasy chains as they interact with one another.

(2) *Group reminiscences.* Group fantasies tend to be remembered because they are always accompanied by high feelings, emotions, and excitement. Other events occur to the group which impress themselves on the members and which they recall in their discussions.

On one occasion a student group was meeting in the evening in a campus building. One member had to come late and found the building locked. The resulting problems and the final solution caused considerable excitement for the group, and they often remembered the event when reminiscing about their common experiences. Whenever a group develops inside jokes or nicknames resulting from fantasy themes that have chained out or because of unusual happenings or adventures, they begin to feel part of an identifiable group.

(3) *Group rites and rituals.* Sometimes the group will do things related to their fantasies and their history over and over again

until they take on the characteristics of rites and rituals. Repeating the action makes the past experience live again to some extent. One student group was in the process of developing cohesion and finding places for the members in the group's role structure when a member pulled a candy bar out of her purse and offered to share it with the rest. Another member in a clowning mood took out a pen knife and made something of an event out of cutting the candy equally and sharing fairly. Subsequently, some member always brought some food to the meeting, and it was always cut into equal portions by the same pen knife and eaten before the members got down to business.

Seven Concrete Steps to Greater Cohesiveness for Your Work Group

Identify your group. Mention your group as a group. Talk about *we, our* group, what *we* hope to accomplish, and how *we* can continue *our* excellent work. Do not accentuate the *I*. The leader should not continually stress such things as, "I want this done," or "I'm asking you to do this as a personal favor to me," or "If you don't do this, I'll find it necessary to . . ." Highly cohesive groups also always work out ways to identify their group; sometimes these are as obvious as insignia, or mascots, or by the use of nicknames.

Build a group tradition. No sooner is a group clearly identified than things happen to it. Fantasies chain out and are remembered. The unit begins to have a history. Unusual, exciting, or funny things can become a part of its history and tradition. The leader can build cohesiveness by recalling these events in group meetings because such recollections emphasize the fact that the group exists through time. Highly cohesive work groups have traditional events or ceremonies that give the unit added meaning and build loyalty. Highly cohesive families have such traditions that help them celebrate certain holidays or special occasions in the family's history.

Stress teamwork. Accept the basic principle of professional athletic teams. Simply put, it is: I don't care if I star so long as we win. Television sports-casters interviewing a home-run hitter will often ask, "How many home runs are you going to hit this year?" A good team player always replies, "I don't care just so long as we win the pennant." Don't worry about who gets the credit so long as your group succeeds.

Get the group to recognize good work. Encourage the group to fulfill the social and esteem needs of one another. The leader can watch his group for compliments being paid, offers to help each other with outside projects, even the simple social recognition of a member by offers of a ride home or invitations to coffee. When these occur, the wise participant or leader will encourage them and add his own compliment, always praising work in terms of the importance of the contribution to the group. Too often, the leader becomes preoccupied with the high status members, but it is the quiet, nonparticipating member who has the greatest need for social and esteem rewards. Too often the attention paid to the low status member is negative. Criticism of his lack of interest, or knowledge, or participation will only make matters worse. A little positive attention to the marginal individual, the potential "dead wood," will go a long way toward increasing group cohesiveness.

Set clear, attainable group goals. Your work group may have some general long-term goals, but a goal several months in the future is too vague for building cohesiveness. A goal for a given meeting, for this week, for next week, is much more likely to increase morale. Achieving a goal rewards the group. Making daily or weekly progress provides such rewards regularly. Of course, if the goal is to be useful, it must be clearly specified and understood by all, and *it must be within reach.* The miler who sees the finish line and thinks he can catch the leader puts on a burst of speed.

Give group rewards. Reaching a clear goal is a group reward in itself, but the leader or supervisor can emphasize the identity of the group, help build a tradition, and stress teamwork by giving the *entire* group a common reward for achieving a goal. Too many organizations have geared their *entire* incentive system to the old view of managing individuals. Individual incentives have been stressed over group incentives. If a coach encouraged every player to be a star — to look out only for himself and cut down every other man on his team — that coach would be in trouble. That team would be in trouble.

One need not give up individual incentives to make wise use of group rewards. These may be monetary or they may be rewards aimed at the needs for esteem and workmanship. Letters of commendation for the group, plaques, dinners, or other social affairs in recognition of a group job well done, these all help.

If a leader or supervisor receives personal recognition such as a special award or letter of commendation, he should call a meeting of his group and reflect this recognition back on them. The old, "I could not have done it without each and every one of you" speech is given so often because it is important to the cohesiveness of the group and because it is, simply, true.

Treat members like people, not machines. The clean precision and absolute efficiency of a highly tooled machine is often taken as the ideal for the workings of a group or the conduct of a meeting. Many organizations would function much more smoothly if the people in them were standard replaceable predictable parts such as those that fit in our mass-produced automobiles. People trained in science and technology often try to work with groups as they work with machines. When they do, the situation often explodes in their faces. Frequently they respond by charging that others are unreasonable because a sensible blueprint for action has been rejected or sabotaged. Human response is difficult to predict. People are not computers. Several decades ago time-and-motion-study engineers developed much more efficient by-the-numbers ways of doing routine jobs. When they tried to get people to adopt these new ways, the workers resisted, and the result was not greater efficiency but less. One large cause of wasted time and inefficiency in the modern organization is the feeling of many of its members that they are cogs in a large and inhuman machine and that nobody recognizes them as human beings who amount to something.

Building A Positive Social Climate

When a new work group starts. In this section we are going to deal with the principles of getting a committee meeting, business conference, or discussion group off on the right foot. These principles can also be used in dealing with more permanent groups, but they are easier to study in newly formed units.

When the members of a new group meet for the first time, they begin to interact socially. They nod or talk to one another. They smile, frown, and laugh. All of these things help build a climate that is pleasant, congenial, and relaxed, or one that is cold, stiff, and tense. A positive social climate makes for an attractive group; it builds cohesiveness by providing social rewards, and it encourages people to speak up and say what they really mean.

Professor Robert Bales and his associates at Harvard University have determined that three types of concrete actions build a good social feeling and three opposite actions build a negative climate. Our discussion is based upon the research from Harvard with modifications from our own research at the University of Minnesota. The positive actions are shows of solidarity, tension release, and agreement. The negative actions are shows of antagonism, tension, and disagreement.

Show solidarity. Any action or statement that indicates to the others that the new group is important is a show of solidarity. Raising another's status, offering to help do something for the group, volunteering, or indicating you are willing to go out of your way and make a personal sacrifice for the group shows solidarity.

The negative side to solidarity is to show antagonism to the group or to another person. While shows of solidarity build a pleasant spirit and rapport, shows of antagonism make the others uncomfortable.

Deal with social tensions. People in new groups always feel a certain amount of tension. Feelings of embarrassment, shyness, and uneasiness when meeting strangers are shows of social tension.

(1) *Primary tensions.* When the discussion group first meets, everyone will experience *primary* tensions. They feel ill at ease. They do not know what to say or how to begin. The first meeting is tense and cold and must be warmed up. When groups experience primary tension, the people speak very softly; they sigh, and they are very polite. They seem bored and uninterested. No person is really bored when he has an opportunity to speak up and make a name for himself. However, every individual gambles a great deal by plunging into the meeting, by taking an active part. He may make a good showing. The others may be impressed by his ability and decide they like him as a person, *but* they may be irritated by him. They may decide he is stupid and uninformed; they may reject him. This gamble makes a person feel nervous and tense, and he may take flight from the situation by pretending he is not interested. Do not be misled. The person who seems bored and uninterested is really very tense and most interested, particularly in the social dimension of the group. If the meeting never releases

the primary tension, the whole style of future meetings may be set in this uncomfortable mold. It is vital that the primary tension be released early! Tension is released through indications of pleasure such as smiles, chuckles, and laughs. Spend some time joking and socializing before getting down to business. Judiciously used, a bit of socializing is time wisely spent. Once the primary tension is released, however, the group should go to work. Waiting too long to get started will waste time. The leader should develop a sense of timing as to the appropriate time to quit the social chit-chat and get on with the job.

(2) *Secondary tensions.* Once people relax and get down to work, new and different social tensions are generated by role struggles, disagreements over ideas, and personality conflicts. Secondary tensions are louder than primary ones. People speak rapidly, they interrupt one another, are impatient to get the floor and have their say; they may get up and pace the room or pound the table. When secondary tensions reach a certain level, the group finds it difficult to concentrate on its job. When that point is reached, the tensions should be released by humor, direct comment, or conciliation. Secondary tensions are more difficult to bleed off than primary ones. There are no easy solutions, but they should not be ignored! By all means, bring them out into the open and talk them over.

Show agreement. Agreement is one of the basic social rewards. Agreements are like money in the bank that buys social status and esteem rewards. When the group agrees with a member, they tender him social currency. They say: we value you. When the others agree with us, we lose our primary tension; we loosen up; we get excited; we take a more active part in the meeting. The more people agree, the more they communicate with one another.

Disagreements serve as negative climate builders. When people disagree, they grow cautious and tense. *Disagreements are socially punishing but absolutely essential to good group work.* They are double-edged. They are necessary to sound thinking. Yet, disagreements always contain an element of personal attack. The person who finds his ideas subjected to rigorous testing and disagreement feels like he is being "shot down."

Successful discussion groups studied at Minnesota worked out ways to tolerate and even encourage disagreements. *None of them, however, managed to keep the disagreements from straining the social fabric.* One of the reasons that the number of disagreements goes up with a rise in cohesiveness is that groups must develop enough cohesiveness to afford disagreements and still not break up. The rate of disagreements is often highest in the family — the most cohesive unit in our society. How often someone complains, "You're so much nicer with strangers than with the members of your own family!"

Some people try to cushion the hurt in a disagreement by saying things like, "That's a good idea, BUT . . .", or, "That's right. I agree with you, BUT . . ." Eventually the others discover that these prefatory agreements or compliments are just ways of setting them up for the knife. They begin to cringe as the ". . . BUT I think we ought to look at the other side of it . . ." hits them. The fact is, *a disagreement, to do its job, must be perceived as a disagreement.* Disagreements are the scalpels the group uses to cut out undesirable ideas, faulty reasoning, and poor evidence. They must be understood to mean: *stop, this will not do.* When they are thus understood, no amount of kind words of introduction will serve to sugarcoat them.

Develop ways to encourage and tolerate disagreements. First, build cohesiveness. Second, do things to knit the group back together after a period of heavy disagreement. Often disagreements increase as the group moves toward a decision. Good groups have built cohesiveness to tolerate and encourage such disagreements, and they use the positive climate builders to knit the group back together after the decision is reached. They joke and laugh. They show solidarity. They say, "It was a good meeting." "It accomplished something." and, "Let's all get behind this decision." They compliment the persons who advocated the rejected plan. They tell them they are needed, that the group cannot succeed without their help.

Another technique sometimes used by successful work groups is to make one person the "disagreer." He tests most of the ideas, and the group expects him to do so. Whenever they feel the need for disagreement, they turn to him. They reward him by giving him a nickname or by joshing him about how disagreeable he is. If a new person joins the group and asks another after the meeting. "What's with him? He's sure disagreeable," the other member would say, "Oh, don't mind Joe. He's just that way. He doesn't mean any harm.

He's really a good guy; he just disagrees with everything." Since Joe plays the role of the person who always disagrees, someone finding his ideas under attack from Joe would be less hurt than he would be under the usual conditions. After all, Joe disagrees with everybody and means no harm.

A Brief Review of Key Ideas from Part I

* The task-oriented small group is composed of three or more people working together to do a clearly specified job or to reach a common goal.

* Five is an excellent number for a work group.

* The first question in the minds of every person in a new work group is: How do I relate to these other people as a human being?

* Cohesiveness encourages productivity, morale, and communication.

* Role specialization in small work groups is inevitable. Role is a person's place in the group—the part he expects to play and the others expect him to play.

* A member's role is worked out jointly by the person and the group.

* Every new group must go through a "shakedown cruise" during which roles are tested. During this "shakedown cruise," secondary tensions mount.

* Although some roles are established quickly and easily, the role of leader is among the last to emerge. (Part II goes into this much more thoroughly.)

* Groups experience a dramatic increase in cohesiveness when their role structure becomes stable. They are then able to get on with their work more effectively.

* Groups develop norms or standard operating procedures dealing with both the task dimension and with social interactions.

* One of the most important features of group dynamics is the power of nonverbal and verbal communication to get people to act as others in the group do.

* As the group develops higher levels of cohesiveness, the pressure on group members to adopt the group's norms increases.

* Like individual habits, the group's norms can be changed.

* Unsatisfied needs are motivators of behavior.

* A little positive attention to the marginal individual, the potential "dead wood," will go a long way toward increasing cohesiveness.

* When primary or secondary tensions reach a certain level, the group finds it difficult to concentrate on its job. Tensions must be released, directly, or indirectly.

* Agreement is one of the most basic social rewards.

* Disagreements are socially punishing but absolutely essential to good group work. A disagreement, to do its job, must be perceived as a disagreement.

* Good groups use the positive climate builders after a decision is reached.

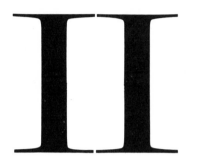

Part II

Objectives

After you have studied Part II you should be able to:

* *observe the communication of members in newly formed groups and discover when the first phase of leadership contention is finished.*

* *note which members have been eliminated as leaders in the first phase.*

* *examine the contenders for leadership in the second phase, and if you are eliminated, select a good time to become a lieutenant for the best of those contending.*

* *if you are a contender in the second phase, read the verbal and nonverbal communication from the members to discover the type and style of leadership they want.*

* *respond quickly to situations as they arise in a meeting in a way that aids the group in reaching its common objective.*

* *exhibit role functions as an appointed leader or moderator that enable you to emerge as the natural as well as the formal leader of the group.*

Leadership

PART II BUILDS UPON YOUR general understanding of group process and development, concentrating upon the role of leadership. Like so many of our everyday ideas about working with groups, leadership often means many different things to different people. Part II examines the various important meanings for leadership and concentrates on reporting results of study and research on the emergence of natural leaders and on the nature of formal leadership. This section deals with such questions as: How do natural leaders emerge in small task-oriented groups? What can I do to become the natural leader of my group? What is the relationship between being appointed a chairman or moderator (formal leadership) and being the natural leader of a group?

The Role of the Leader

We are of two minds. Of all the roles that emerge in a work group, none has fascinated the philosophers, writers, social scientists, and the man on the street more than the top role, the top position. The high status, most influential role has been the subject of novels, dramas, poetry, conjecture, old wives' tales, folklore, and, of late, many scientific investigations.

When we talk of this role in common sense terms we usually refer to it as the *leadership role.* In our country we are of two minds about leadership. If a member of a test tube group suggests that another person would be a good leader, the typical response is, "Oh, no! Not me. Someone else could do a better job." Despite such protests, nearly every member of the groups when interviewed said he (or she) would actually like to have been the leader, to have had his way, to have run things.

Why this ambivalence? On the one hand, our democratic traditions suggest that all men are created equal and that nobody is better than anybody else. We maintain a belief in a classless society. The candidate for office makes much of being an uncommon common man. He is just one of the folks, and he likes baseball, hunting, fishing, and hot dogs. The candiate does not even *seek* office. Only an egotist would publicly assert that he is better than other men and so deserves the job. Rather, he waits for a draft and when he is called, he humbly and modestly does his best to live up to "the high responsibility and great challenge." On the other hand, we love success. Top status positions are symbols of success. We work hard to get to the top. Young men, and increasingly with the rise of Women's Liberation young women, too, are expected to be a success and make something of themselves. They are educated for leadership, trained for leadership, and encouraged to become leaders.

The "now I want it, now I don't" feeling about leadership explains why we spend so much time investigating and studying leadership. Investigators have explained leadership by three major approaches: (1) the trait approach, (2) the styles of leadership approach, and (3) the contextual approach.

The trait approach. The earliest tradition of leadership assumes that leaders are born and not made. Leadership is inherent in the person, and he is destined to become a leader. In early times he was chosen of God or the gods; in more recent times he was thought to have the proper leadership traits. In the early years of the century, social scientists explored the traits a person had to have in order to become a leader. They measured all sorts of characteristics to see if they were related to leadership. They measured the weight and height of leaders and nonleaders. They gave vocabulary, intelligence, and personality tests to many people. In 1948, Professor R. M. Stogdill, a psychologist, published a study entitled "Personal Factors Associated with Leadership: A Survey of the Literature." He was unable to find in all the studies any pattern of inherent personality traits that would explain leadership. The notion that leaders are born and not made just did not stand up under careful and systematic study.

The styles of leadership approach. Next, the students of leadership investigated the question of whether or not they could find an ideal style of leadership. Much of the work was done in organizational settings, particularly in business and industry. Researchers examined authoritarian, democratic, and *laissez-faire* (hands off) styles of leadership. They compared autocratic with democratic, group-centered with leader-centered, production-oriented with employee-oriented leadership and management. One school of industrial psychologists and management experts developed an approach to *participative* management which was essentially democratic management. The first results seemed to indicate clear superiority in terms of morale and productivity for the democratic style of leadership. Nevertheless, as more research accumulated, some groups were found to do well with a more directive or authoritarian style. The surgeon in the operating room was authoritarian; so was the football coach. Clearly, the purpose of the group and the kind of work it had to do played a part in determining the best "style" of leadership for that particular group.

The contextual approach. The most satisfactory explanation of leadership is furnished by the approach that says leadership is a result of the individual traits (inherited characteristics plus training), the purposes of the group; the pressures put on the group from the outside, and the way the persons in the group talk, work, and relate with one another. This view recognizes that some people learn to play the game of "being leader" and that they tend to have certain opening moves that they use in starting the game whenever they join a new work group. To some extent, the way they try to be leader depends upon what they think about the group. They do not approach the squad at basic training in the army with the same expectations that they do a peer discussion group. The sergeant tends to be "bossy," while the moderator of the discussion group tends to be democratic. Our approach is the contextual view, and the test tube groups explain the way a *leader* emerges during the course of a group working on a job. Such an explanation provides a more complete view of leadership than either the trait approach or the one-best-style approach. It includes the idea that leaders are to some extent "born," but it also suggests that potential leaders can achieve skills and improve talents. The contextual approach, the consideration of the total context, or all components, of each instance of "a group," explains why a man who emerges as leader in one group may fail to emerge as the leader of a second apparently similar group. It also accounts for successful groups that follow leaders who have quite different styles of leadership.

The Way Leaders Emerge

The method of residues. If we dip a glass of water from the ocean and allow it to stand until the water evaporates, the salt that is left is a *residue.* If we try to pick out the salt before the water evaporates, we have quite a job. In like fashion the group does not pick a leader. Rather, it eliminates people from consideration until one person is left. The test tube groups select their leaders *by the method of residues.*

The one outstanding feature of the reports people make of the early meetings of a work group is that while they cannot say who will emerge as the leader, they have little difficulty agreeing on who will *not* be the leader. People look first for clues that will eliminate others from high-status roles. Ruling people out helps them concentrate their attention on the remaining contenders. Moreover when someone picks another as a potential leader, he has to shut the door on his own hopes. People like to leave that door open.

The general pattern of the way leaders emerge consists of two phases. The first is relatively short. During this time, the group eliminates people who are clearly unsuitable. The second is much longer and during this phase, the remaining serious contenders battle it out for support.

The first phase. In case studies at the University of Minnesota, roughly one-half of the participants were ruled out in the first phase. First to go were those who "did not take part." Next, the group eliminated those who, though active, seemed uninformed, ignorant, or unskilled at the task. It was felt these members did not know much, or that they "didn't make much sense." And finally, some very active and vociferous participants were eliminated because they took strong, unequivocal stands. They expressed their position in flat, unqualified assertions, and impressed upon the others that they would not change their minds no matter what. They were perceived as being "too extreme" or "too inflexible."

Phase two. The second part of the process was characterized by intensified competition among the remaining members. Members felt irritated and frustrated. The group was wasting time and "nothing was accomplished." This was the toughest part of the "shakedown cruise." Animosities developed among some of the participants. The group began to run away from the question of leadership. Sometimes they found scapegoats to account for their failures. Too much was expected of them, they'd say. The upper echelon didn't understand their problems. Someone else was to blame outside the group. At other times they blamed some one member for their problems. Often they reported that nothing could be done to improve the group. They were victims of circumstances or of an unfortunate, inherent, unchangeable set of personality traits lodged in certain members. Secondary tensions rose to uncomfortable levels.

To illustrate the way groups select leaders, we will outline two typical and successful paths that many groups used to steer a course through the second phase.

(1) *Path one.* The first is a relatively short and easy way through the struggle for leadership. We will use the basic group composed of Joe, Harry, Bill, Don, and Wilbur. Let us say that Joe is eliminated because he is quiet, and Don is eliminated because he seems uninformed. Wilbur has assumed the role of tension releaser and is thus eliminated as a potential leader. This concludes the first phase. Bill and Harry remain in contention. During the second phase, as both try to give orders and divide up work, Joe decides that Harry is capable but arbitrary and tactless. He finds Bill capable,

sensible, and understanding. Joe begins to support Bill whenever Bill makes a leadership move. He voices his support. He *agrees* and says, "That's a good idea. Let's do it that way." At this point, Joe emerges in the role of *lieutenant*. The emergence of a lieutenant is a key development in determining leadership. Bill, if he gains a strong lieutenant, is in a much better position to emerge as a leader.

After another period of contention, Wilbur begins to side with Bill and Joe. In short order, Don swings over and Bill has emerged as leader. When this happens the group will experience a considerable release of social tension and a corresponding increase in cohesiveness. Not all of their role problems have been solved, however. Harry is a potential source of trouble. He may be upset enough to try to sabotage the group. He is one of the more capable members or he would not have remained in contention in the second phase. When he loses his bid for leadership he is frustrated and upset. He usually finds Bill personally obnoxious and is irritated with Joe for supporting Bill's ideas. Bill and Harry typically are in the midst of a personality conflict.

Good groups knit people like Harry back into the group in a productive, useful, and high status role such as a task expert or an information-source person. Many groups failed at this crucial point. The newly emerged leader often has considerable animosity for the loser. Bill will typically find Harry unreasonable and troublesome. He thinks of Harry as a potential source of trouble. The greatest mistake that he can make at this point is to give in to the human tendency to exploit the power of his new role as leader to make life miserable for Harry. If Bill does "rub Harry's nose in it," he can expect trouble as long as Harry remains in the group. Bill should remember that *the newly emerged leader is always on probation. If he does not work out, he will be deposed.* Some of the new leaders who punished their opponents lost their positions because of this. The others decided that if that was the way the leader dealt with the opposition, they did not want him for their leader. The wise leader, with support from his lieutenant and the others, always took pains at this crucial point to support the loser and to encourage him in another productive role.

(2) *Path two.* The second way to finding a leader is more frustrating and difficult than the first. We will return to our basic group at the point where Bill gained a lieutenant, Joe. Had the group taken path two, at this point Wilbur would have found Harry's style of leading more to his liking than Bill's. Perhaps Wilbur has a greater appreciation for Harry's wry humor, and he finds that Harry's skill in thinking through problems more than compensates for his bluntness. Wilbur thus becomes Harry's *lieutenant.* Now the group works two against two with Don becoming the "swing vote." Such groups may continue the second phase for a long time before Don casts a consistent deciding vote. In one of the case studies at Minnesota, the group continued for several weeks deadlocked in this fashion until one of the contenders turned to the swing vote and asked him directly, "Where do you stand?" The member replied, "Right in the middle." Of course, the struggle continued.

If the problems become too frustrating, the members may decide that they lack leadership; so they hold an election. If the group is not ready to really follow either Harry or Bill, they will take flight from the leadership struggle by electing someone who was eliminated in the first phase — perhaps a quiet woman, or in the case of our prototype group, they would probably elect Don because he is neutral. People in Don's position, when elected leader, will usually accept the job and *begin acting like a leader.* No matter how quiet and uninvolved their manner has been up to that point, they change drastically and begin to take charge. The others do not follow, however, and within a short period of time, Don will cease to act like a leader, and Bill and Harry will continue the contention until Don swings his support to Bill. Wilbur's move at this juncture is crucial. Should he stay committed to Harry, the group may be doomed to work without clear leadership or stable roles. However, Wilbur has demonstrated a preoccupation with social matters, and he is alert to the secondary tensions. Since he is a buddy of Harry's, he is in an excellent position to swing his support to Bill, joke away the tensions, and conciliate Harry into a productive role.

The Lessons of Leadership Emergence

The yardstick for leadership is the group's goal. The members spend time and energy on leadership because it is so important to the success of the group. We are very touchy about the people who "boss" us around. We do not like to take orders. If we have to, we prefer a leader who gives wise orders in a way we can tolerate. The leader will make crucial suggestions and decisions about the way the work will be divided and the way the material resources of the group will be distributed. In the end, the group rejects potential leaders until they are left with the person who seems best able to lead *for the good of all.*

In some groups leaders fail to emerge. Sometimes the struggle for leadership is never resolved. Such groups become invalids. The members spend their time in backbiting and getting back at internal enemies. If after the first phase a group is left with two or three potential leaders, each having substantial handicaps, the leadership may not be resolved. For example, one group was left with two persons in contention. One had a strong aggressive style of organizing the work. He took charge and "came on strong." He was perceived as being too dictatorial and bossy. The other was much more congenial and less aggressive. He had more understanding of the esteem and social needs of the group. However, the group soon discovered that, though he had definite human relations skills, his thinking was fuzzy and tentative. He also proved to be indecisive. The first man was clearly the more capable of the two in developing coherent courses of action, but . . . On balance, the two contenders were equally handicapped. As a result, the group was unwilling to follow either.

Central persons. Some people have developed opening moves as they search for a role in a new work group that fascinate the others. They may be positive or negative people; we shall call them *central* persons. A central person may be a "star." He may be unusually capable and a potential asset to the group's productivity, or he may be exceptionally skillful at human relations, unusually charming. A central person who would be a great threat to the group would be a member who seems extremely hostile to the group and its purposes or someone who downgrades the work. He may make it plain he feels the others in the group are incapable. At any rate, his attitude becomes a central concern to the group. Sometimes a central person is someone who is unusually apathetic and uninvolved, who simply refuses to take part in the group. All of these people tend to take the group's attention away from its tasks.

A common threatening central person is the *manipulator*. He comes to the group with the intention of exploiting it for his own ends. He intends to take it over and run it. Manipulators tend to be either *hard sell* or *soft sell*. The hard sell manipulator usually comes on strong. He talks a great deal and takes charge immediately with a strong hand. "Let's get down to business. Now here's what we will do." When the group resists his leadership, he tries to argue and browbeat the others into line. When someone challenges him, the others will swing to support the contender. Often the hard sell manipulator then stands alone against the group, trying hard to talk everyone down. On other occasions, the hard sell manipulator finds no one who will challenge him immediately. He then is certain that he has succeeded in taking over. When he gives orders, however, they are not followed. People continually misunderstand, or they fail to follow through. He decides that he has not been "working hard enough," at his leading, so he begins to give his orders slowly, carefully, in simple English as though he were talking to morons. This arouses even greater resentment and "goldbricking." He decides that they are all lazy and irresponsible. Inevitably, another contender emerges and becomes leader. The manipulator is now extremely frustrated. His self-image is badly dented. He came into the group confident of his superiority and his ability to run the group "his way," and the group has rejected him. He seldom examines where he has failed. Usually he turns on the group; they are ignorant and stupid. If he remains in the group, he is often a troublemaker. Finding him an acceptable role takes ingenuity.

The soft sell manipulator is often much more successful in his second phase. He often emerges for a time as the leader. He has many "tricks" and "formulas" of human relations at his command. He is friendly and congenial. He seems less bossy and more democratic. He sizes up the group to see whom he can "con" and who will be troublesome for him. He does more work outside the group's formal meetings, like chatting with this or that member over coffee. He is a "politician." After several weeks of working together, however, the others find him out. They discover that he is getting his way and that under his apparently congenial and democratic facade, he is using the group for his personal ends. When the soft sell manipulator is found out, a challenger comes forward, and the group must reshuffle roles until a new leader emerges.

Effect of changing personnel. In some test tube groups a new member was deliberately introduced after a leader had emerged and the roles stabilized. In others, a member was removed, and in still others, a member was removed and a new person inserted in his place. In all instances, a change in personnel proved unsettling. If a new person was added, this person brought with him a complement of skills and talents, and a role had to be found for him. All of the roles had to be reshuffled to free enough of the duties to form a slot for the new man. When a member was removed, a role struggle also resulted. His tasks had to be assumed by the remaining members. If he had important duties, the members who stood to gain by *climbing* upward on the status ladder came into conflict. Likewise when a member was replaced, the new man did not take over the same role that the former person had; more reshuffling of all roles was necessary.

The effect of changing personnel by adding, removing, or replacing individuals is a repeat of the "shakedown cruise." The typical result is a period of role instability and struggle that surprises and frustrates the members. People often do not understand what is going on and why it must go on. They respond by blaming the new member. "Everything was fine until he came." Or they bemoan the loss of a member. "Before John left, everything went along fine; we sure miss John."

Effect of appointing a leader. What happens to the test tube groups when one of the members is appointed the leader? This is an extremely important question because so many work groups have an appointed supervisor, foreman, chief, manager, head, chairman, or boss. Appointing a leader had three interesting effects on, but did not change, the *fundamental* pattern of leader emergence.

(1) *Appointed leader takes over.* The appointed leader immediately *began to act like a leader.* At first the group looked to the appointed leader for leadership. However, after he had

led for a time and they had followed in a tentative way, his leadership was challenged by one or two of the other members. The challenge came at the end of the first phase of the leadership struggle. This was a turning point for the appointed leader. If he acted hurt and thought that because he was appointed leader they ought to follow him, he was well on his way to being rejected.

(2) *The role struggle facilitated.* When after a brief challenge the appointed leader demonstrated he was a good choice for the job, the members quickly followed his lead and the second phase of the leadership struggle was short and easy. If the appointed leader was the person who would have emerged as natural leader of the group, assigning him the job made the "shakedown cruise" much smoother.

(3) *The role struggle prolonged.* The third effect of assigning a leader was to slow down the process of having a natural leader emerge. In such a case, the assigned leader took charge, was followed, then challenged, was deposed, and a new leadership struggle began. The "shakedown cruise" was long and rough for these groups. The assigned leader had lost his position and esteem. The group had to find a productive role for him or be plagued with a disgruntled member in a formal position of leadership.

Seven Concrete Steps to Natural Leadership

From the Minnesota Studies of test tube groups we have developed a profile of the talk and action that often resulted in a member emerging as leader. You should understand that even if you talk and act this way in a given group, it is no guarantee that you will become the natural leader. Another member may do and say these things in a way the others in the group find more to their liking. However, people who do not understand groups really seldom do or say very many of these things at all. Here, conscious competence leads to success because so few people realize how natural leaders emerge in work groups.

Do not be a manipulator. The most certain way to assure being eliminated as a leader is to act and talk in such a way that the others perceive that you are attempting to manipulate them or the group.

We all belong to groups in which we have a sincere interest. We are dedicated to their welfare and feel no desire to manipulate them. A good salesman knows that he must be sold on his product to sell it to others. The member who emerges as the natural leader must be sincerely and completely dedicated to the welfare of the group.

Be willing to pay the price. To emerge as the natural leader you must want to help the group enough to do the work. Almost everyone would like the rewards of leadership, but not every member is willing to work "above and beyond the call of duty" for the good of all. People who emerge as leaders make personal sacrifices for the group. They work overtime, inconvenience themselves, and tackle even low status tasks with enthusiasm. Members who emerge as leaders are willing to arouse resentment and take criticism. The group requires that its leader make some of the tough decisions. Harry Truman said of the Presidency, "The buck stops here." Certainly this is true of work groups. When painful decisions about distributing rewards unequally, for example, must be made, the group usually pushes them on the leader. Such decisions inevitably arouse resentment. The person who emerges as leader must demonstrate that he is tough enough to make such decisions wisely and take the criticism.

Talk up. If you wish to be leader, you must take an active interest in the group's work. You must make a contribution. Your talk and action must show an active commitment to the group, a concern and consideration for the others as people, and an understanding of the task. Remember, however, that the person who talks a lot but who seems to be a manipulator, or who seems inflexible, or uninformed, does not emerge as leader.

Do your homework. If you wish to be a leader you must know what is going on. Members who emerge as leaders have sensible ideas and state them clearly. They know things that will help the group. Be informed about the group's work. Plan for the good of the group. Put in extra time working out ways to improve the group and to help it achieve its goals. Members who emerge as leaders demonstrate that they can provide workable and efficient plans of action.

Make personal sacrifices. Nothing tells the others more clearly that you are sincere and not a manipulator than your willingness to make personal sacrifices for the group. The manipulator gets his way at the expense of the group. The natural leader gets the group's way at his personal expense. Volunteering to aid the group or to help members work for the group is evidence of your sincerity. Members who emerge as leaders do not worry about who gets credit for work or for ideas. They often give credit offered to them to others. People who worry about recognition that *their* plan, or *their* way, or *their* ideas are used seldom emerge as leaders.

Raise the status of other members. Closely related to the fact that leaders do not worry about getting credit for their work is their tendency to raise the status of other members. They compliment other people when they do something for the group. They indicate that every person in the group is significant and is making a contribution. They seek out ways to make other people feel important. In short, you are more likely to emerge as an esteemed leader if you forget about it and work as hard as you can to make the group a good one.

Build group cohesiveness. In Part I we suggested seven steps (pages 32-34) to build cohesiveness. Members who emerge as leaders do many of these things. They communicate their interest in the group and its welfare. They help build a history and a tradition.

Formal Leadership

Test tube groups and real life groups. Most of our groups are not composed of peers and everyone does not start out equal. Most work groups function within a *formal* organization. The salesman works *under* a sales manager within a corporation. Student governments have presidents and their committees have chairmen. The executive committee of the PTA chapter functions within the larger organization. People come to such work groups with different status. Sometimes the status is internal to the organization, such as the dean meeting with a group of students. Sometimes the status is external to the group, such as having a famous surgeon and a famous financier meeting on the same committee for the campus development fund. Although such status differences introduce complications, the basic process of group development can be adjusted to take these into account. In other words, test tube groups do tell us about real life meetings, about real life groups. We haven't time to make applications to all the many variations of work groups, but we will show the way leadership emergence is related to the management of organizational work groups. With this application as a guide you can make similar modifications of the principles to fit other situations.

Formal position. Organizations usually have a formal structure. Members simply do not have enough contact with all other people in a large organization to form impressions about them. Certainly they do not work together enough to develop a role structure. *Formal positions* take the place of roles and tell a given person what the organization expects from him and what he can expect from the organization. The formal positions may be blue-printed into a table of organization:

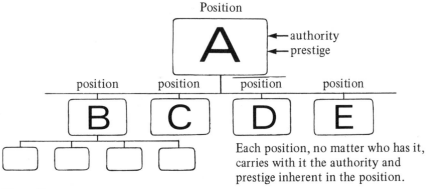

Each position, no matter who has it, carries with it the authority and prestige inherent in the position.

Figure 2

Figure 2 is part of a typical table of organization. The duties of each position may be written out so that each person who fills that position knows what he must do *and* what he must not do. The status relationships are spelled out as well. The bigger the box and the closer to the top, the higher the status of the position. Each position has certain tasks associated with it. No matter who fills box A, he is expected to hire and fire the people in boxes B, C, D, and E. He may have the duty of making and implementing plans. The position will also carry the right to reward or punish those in positions below. The duties can be thought of as *responsibilities.* If the duties are not taken care of, the organization will call the person in the position to account. Associated with the duties and sanctions of each position is a certain amount of *authority*. The authority goes with the position and is inherited by every man who takes it over. A certain amount of *prestige* also goes along with each position. This prestige adheres to every person who fills the formal position.

By placing people in the table of organization, we add new dimensions to the properties inherent in the positions themselves. Power is added to the authority in a certain position, and esteem to

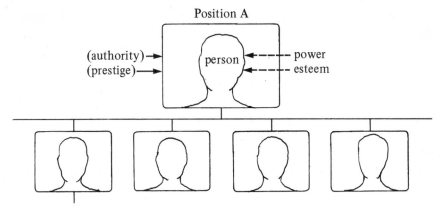

Figure 3

the prestige. Power is the effective exercise of authority and is, thus, a function of the authority inherent in the position plus the role that the person develops in the work groups to which he belongs.

A certain amount of prestige adheres to every person who fills the particular position. However, when a man assumes a position, he begins to work out a role in the informal work groups. In that process he earns a certain amount of *esteem*. Esteem is not inherent in the position; it must be earned. *Thus power and esteem are both parts of the role that a person comes to play in the actual groups* that do the organization's work.

Formal leadership and natural leadership. The formal structure of an organization is static. It is set. The informal work groups that develop and change with a turnover in personnel and with fluctuating working conditions are dynamic. They constantly change, a little, or a lot. Frequently the informal organization, that is, the power and esteem that members earn, departs from the formal organization. The map no longer fits the realities. You cannot tell about a man's power and esteem by finding out his place in the formal table of organization. When formal leadership departs from natural leadership, trouble often follows. The real "boss" may not be the man with the title. What then?

The role struggle between a man with the formal position to help him in his battle for control and a man with the esteem and power furnished by his standing with the members can be long and bloody. One example will show how group process applies to the problems of formal leadership. Let's say that a person in a position of formal leadership leaves the organization and a new man takes his place. Assume that the replacement is a stranger to the members in the work group. The entire role structure of that group will undergo a "shakedown cruise!"

The new manager must assume certain leadership functions for the work group because the formal position says that he must. He is expected by top management and by the organization to lead his group immediately. He will not, however, be accepted as the natural leader of the group without a period of testing. He must find his role in the informal groups within his department according to the basic principles of group process. When he finally assumes his role, it will be slightly different from that of the former manager, and the whole group will experience a reshuffling of roles. He does have certain standard levers furnished by the organization to help him emerge as leader. These may include increasing salaries, giving bonuses, promoting, assigning jobs and vacations, the right to punish tardiness, malingering, and poor work. You may think that these levers give the new man an insurmountable advantage. Wisely used by a person who understands the dynamics of small groups, they may. Sometimes, however, the authority to punish and reward members turns out to be a handicap rather than a help.

Here is how it might happen. The new manager, whoever he is, is a marked man! His boss is watching closely to see how he will work out. He tries to do an exceptionally good job. The members of the group watch him even more carefully. Will he turn out to be a man they can follow? If he begins with strong and decisive leadership moves, he can expect some resistance. He may also find that he is misunderstood. Misunderstanding directions is a common way of resisting an order. To a man on trial, eager to prove his efficiency, such response may lead to frustration and anger. The new manager has now come to a crucial point. If he controls his anger and asks, "What have I done wrong . . . ?" he may be able to go back and mend his fences and start to build a role of leadership within the group. If he understands the way people emerge as natural leaders, he may win the power and esteem that the authority and prestige of his job deserve and without which he must remain ineffective and unsatisfied to some extent. If he lashes back and pulls the levers by which he can force members to obey, he will start a spiral effect that results in malingering, more crises, less work, and trouble with his superiors. If he panics and decides that the trouble with his group is that he has not been firm enough, he may wildly put pressure on his people. He will lay down the law, read off the lazy workers, make sure that his directions are crystal clear, and supervise the most minute details of the work.

The members of his unit will then reject him as their leader, and someone else will emerge as the natural leader—the one to whom they all go with their gripes. Any new manager who starts down this toboggan ride will soon reach a point where more of his time and energy will be devoted to internal crises and struggling with members of his group than to his work. Such groups disturb their members. The morale declines. Members have difficulty talking about anything but their troubles. They vent their spleen on "him" and on any members who have sold out to "him." They plot and plan ways to get back at "him."

Although our example applied the knowledge about the small group to a hypothetical business organization, the same principles apply to the newly elected president of a fraternity or sorority, the chairman of a college department, or the chairman of an urban action group.

A Brief Review of Key Ideas from Part II

* The group does not pick a leader; rather, it eliminates people from consideration until one person emerges as leader.

* The second phase of the leadership struggle is the toughest part of the "shakedown" cruise.

* The emergence of a lieutenant is a key development in determining leadership.

* The newly emerged leader is always on probation. If he does not work out, he will be deposed.

* If a group is forced to elect a leader before they are ready to make this decision, they will take flight by electing a clearly unsuitable leader.

* If a clearly unsuitable leader is appointed or elected, he will begin to act like a leader, but no one will follow him.

* A leader who best serves the needs of the entire group will emerge from the group.

* One of the most negative persons is a manipulator who comes to the group with the intention of exploiting it for his own ends.

* When a group changes personnel, a period of role instability and struggle will follow.

* If an appointed leader is satisfactory, he will emerge as the natural leader after a brief and easy testing time.

* If an appointed leader is unsatisfactory, he will be deposed and a new natural leader will emerge after a long and difficult testing time.

* Leaders cannot be imposed on the group. The leader must earn the right to lead even if he has been appointed a *formal* leader.

* Authority and prestige are associated with a formal position.

* Power and esteem are associated with the person's role in his group as well as his formal position in the organization.

* The formal structure is static; the informal working relationships (the roles) are dynamic.

* When formal leadership departs from natural leadership, trouble often follows.

III

Part III

Objectives

After you have studied Part III you should be able to:

* *describe and evaluate the nonverbal communication in a meeting.*

* *evalute the feedback patterns and communication networks in a meeting.*

* *use Checklist 1, p. 91, to make a good plan for a meeting.*

* *have an approach planned to break the ice and get a meeting started.*

* *respond quickly to situations as they arise to assure the release of primary tension and create a positive social climate.*

* *respond quickly to situations as they arise to provide sufficient structure for the group to achieve its task objective.*

* *respond quickly to situations as they arise which generate secondary tension.*

* *encourage the nonparticipant and draw the quiet person into the group.*

* *discourage the person who speaks too much and still keep the member as a productive participant.*

* *use Checklist 2, p. 92, as a basis for a thorough evaluation of a meeting.*

* *use Checklist 3, p. 93, as a basis for a thorough and clear-eyed evaluation of your own leadership in a meeting.*

Small Group Communication

THIS THIRD SECTION DEALS WITH small group communication and considers such questions as: How do groups make decisions? How can the efficiency of communication be improved? What changes of attitude can aid in developing skills in listening, speaking, and testing ideas. In addition, Part III answers some of the nagging little questions that plague any person who must lead a meeting such as: What task responsibilities do I as a leader have? What should I do to get ready before the meeting? Where is the best place to meet? How can I facilitate communication and save time with the use of questions? By the use of an agenda? What should I do to encourage participation? To discourage the person who dominates the meeting? What should I do to follow up the results of a meeting?

The Process of Communication

Communication. Like group process, communication events are complex. They are also processes which have the give-and-take characteristic of people working together in groups. Let us examine one unit of communication to see its basic parts and how they fit together. Later we will attempt to set them in motion in the give-and-take of the process.

David Berlo has used the letters S-M-C-R as a key to the components of an act of communication. *S* stands for the *source* of the communication. If the college president dictates a memorandum to all department chairmen, he is the source for the communication event. The *M* represents the *message,* the actual words placed on the paper by the president's secretary. The *C* in the formula indicates the *channel* or channels through which the message moves. Most basically, each person receives messages through his senses, sight, smell, taste, hearing, and touch. Thus you are most likely to hear or read a message. Another set of channels consists of such paths as telephone lines, television waves, sound waves, or interoffice mail. The message moves from the source through channels until it reaches the *receiver,* the *R* in S-M-C-R. Thus the president (source) sends a memorandum (message) through intercampus mail (channel) which is read (channel) by department chairman Smith (receiver). The memorandum directs Smith to appear at 3 P.M., Thursday afternoon in conference room A for a meeting. He is told to bring the latest figures on his proposal for new instructional equipment.

The source of the communication usually makes a prediction when he sends out a message. In this case, the president predicts that Professor Smith will appear with the appropriate information at the appropriate time. If Smith fails to appear, the president is disturbed. He calls his secretary and tells her to check on Smith. She is very apologetic; it seems that Smith called in the morning to say he was sick and as the president was busy, she took the message and then forgot to tell him. The point here is that communication events are always parts of chains of communication. No sooner does a receiver get a message than he becomes the source of another message sent back through channels to the first source. Thus, a give-and-take, and interchange of messages back and forth between the people communicating with one another, characterizes the process.

The small group as a message processing system. The work group can be viewed as a message processing system. Much of the work consists of gathering, interpreting, and evaluating messages. The group then produces messages which they send back through channels to other groups and organizations. You can place the entire group into the S-M-C-R formula as a source and receiver of messages. You can also think of each person in the group as the source and receiver of internal messages that result, more or less, in a meeting of the minds within the group. Our concern will be with the internal face-to-face communication.

Nonverbal communication. A common complaint is that too much time is wasted in meetings. Ironically, the time-wasting meeting often results from the *nonverbal* communication that is a by-product of trying to save time. Bill, who called the meeting, bustles into the room a bit late, having hastily spent the last few minutes preparing for the session. "I'm sorry to call you together on such short notice. I know how busy you all are and believe me, I'm running late myself. Sorry, but I got caught on the phone at the last minute and couldn't get away." He glances at his watch, takes it off his wrist and places it on the table before him. "I wouldn't have called this meeting, but something important has come up that we have to handle today. I know some of you have to be out of here by eleven o'clock and I've got a meeting myself, so I assure you we will be out of here by then."

Everything about Bill's manner communicates haste. He glances at his watch. When a discussion develops, he grows restless and looks at the agenda. "I hate to break in," he says, "but we only have about about fifteen more minutes." It takes a brave person to raise a question or start to challenge ideas in such a meeting. The others all get the message; they accept the fact that the most important goal of the meeting actually is to get through the agenda in a hurry. Bill's gestures, posture, facial expressions and vocal tone all send out the message, "hurry, hurry . . ." Those present go through the motions of a meeting. They mention the items on the agenda, but the group is not really having a meeting; no real communication takes place. The meeting may be efficient and speedy, but the discussion does not result in any understanding. Such a meeting, is, indeed, a waste of time.

Nonverbal communication refers to the information conveyed by the way a person talks and acts over and above (or in place of) the message in his words. The way something is said and the actions that accompany it are always more believable than the sentiments expressed by the words. To paraphrase Emerson, the *way* you say it speaks so loudly that I cannot hear what you say. Bill, by glancing at his watch, talking rapidly, and fidgeting, tells his group that he feels the meeting is an imposition on their time and not as important as other matters that they all need to attend to. He may say that "something important has come up," but when he acts like he doesn't really believe this, and when he does not let the group treat it as though it were something important, the others accept the nonverbal message as being more truthful.

The president of a small company once felt that he needed good honest information from his employees. "They know," he said, "that my door is always open." He grew excited. "I have told them again and again that I have an open door policy. Any man who works for me can come right through that door at any time of the day and tell me exactly what he thinks." He was now speaking in a loud voice. "Why is it that nobody ever comes?"

When this question was raised later, in private, with one of the employees, the employee without a word made a knife out of his forefinger, raised it to his throat, and made a cutting motion. The employees of the blustering boss got a powerful nonverbal message from him that cancelled out his verbal plea that his door was "always open."

The success of a meeting hinges upon the proper attitude and commitment of those who organize and conduct it. Unless the leader is sold on the meeting and indicates by word and deed that it is a useful communication tool and that he expects it to accomplish important work, the meeting will often be a waste of time. All through the book we have stressed the importance of nonverbal communication to the development of cohesiveness, stable roles, and good social relations. Insincerity and manipulative moves always get through to the others because of nonverbal cues.

Arousing meanings. Meanings are personal. Meanings, like motives, are in people. *Meanings are not in messages.* No other person has quite the same set of meanings that you have. When he hears the word *mother,* he experiences a different meaning than you do. The problem is to get a community of meaning shared by all members of the work group. How is this done? A person, say, has a meaning he wants the group to share. He cannot put the meaning into words, speak them out of his mouth, have them carry the meaning through the air and into the ear of the listener, and then release precisely that meaning inside the head of the listener. All he can do is send out verbal and nonverbal messages that express his meaning and trust that the receiver will associate similar meanings with the messages. But the odds are very great that the first time he tries to explain himself to the group and get a community of shared meaning, he will fail.

Feedback. Here is the crux of the problem. Unless he gets a message back indicating the extent of his failure, the source of a message *will assume that he has succeeded.* There's an old Spanish saying that he who keeps silent, consents. In the communication process, feedback refers to the questions, comments, facial expressions, and so forth that indicate how much the receiver understands from the message. Feedback is a term borrowed from the study of control instruments. Automation would be impossible without feedback. The principle is contained in the simple thermostat that governs the heat in a room. A desired level is set on the thermostat. It reads the actual temperature and compares it with the desired level. If the actual temperature is too cold, it turns on the furnace; when the desired level of heat is reached, it turns off the furnace. In terms of a work group, a member tells another something. He then watches and listens as the other member provides messages to give the speaker a reading on what the member got out of the message (what meanings it aroused in the receiver). The speaker then compares the desired level of communication with the actual and sends out additional messages designed to bring the communications on target.

For an example, take the case of two sculptors who can talk with one another by telephone but cannot see each other. One is looking at a clay statue. The other is working on a block of granite. The first describes the clay statue to the second. Together they go to work, talking back and forth, trying to get the second sculptor to approximate the clay figure in stone. It is hard work. The man with the hammer and chisel must ask many questions and listen carefully. It will take considerable time and in the end, the stone statue will only be an approximation of the original clay figure.

The speaker and listener in a group are faced with a similar problem; the "statues" are meanings within each person. The source knows his meaning and tries to shape a similar one from the material available (the meanings) within the receiver. In this way, working together, the two come to a meeting of the minds. If the listener does not provide feedback to give a reading on how well the speaker is doing, the communication will fail.

The Problem of Effective Communication

Some do not want to communicate. Not all message sources have successful communication as their basic purpose.

(1) *Some use language to confuse.* They try to beg the question. If they have something to hide they would rather have the others confused than informed.

(2) *Some use language to show off.* They try to gain status as experts by using technical jargon. They prefer not to be questioned.

(3) *Some use language from habit.* They are like robots. Turn them on and certain habitual records begin to play. How are you? Isn't it exciting? The weather has been very nice. How wonderful.

Some fail to provide feedback. Even with the best intentions in the world, communication is difficult.

Recently the Small Group Communication Seminar at Minnesota made intensive case studies of the failure to communicate information. The main problem in this failure turned out to be that *the person who did not know, did not ask.* Very seldom during the first discussions did anyone say, "I'm sorry, but I don't know about that. Could you tell me more?" Studies conducted by Professor Bales at Harvard University which counted every question and every statement in a large number of meetings indicate that group communication is characterized by *answers looking for questions.* The discussions of the Harvard students were composed of about one-third questions and two-thirds answers.

Why don't people provide feedback by asking questions when they don't understand. We already know, of course, that during the struggle for roles, people do not want to appear ignorant and lose face (status) in the group. Often members pretended to know more than they actually did rather than ask for information. Then, too, in some of the meetings, very few questions were raised, so it just did not seem to be the thing to do.

Some fail to listen. During the period of the "shakedown cruise" people often cannot ask a question because they have not listened to the previous comment. During the period of role testing, people are eager to demonstrate their wares. They wait for a cue from the discussion that makes them "think of something to say." They then plan how they will say it and watch impatiently for an opening. When they get the stage, they say as much as they can, as effectively as they can. When they must give up the spotlight, they try to think up another good comment. When one occurs to them, they wait for another opportunity to speak. Since people seldom listen well during the "shakedown cruise," they often say things unrelated to the topic mentioned by the previous person. They say what is on their minds even if the comment is no longer pertinent, and they say as much as they can think of even though they may introduce several ideas within one comment.

If an individual has not done well in a session, he may be disturbed enough to go over the proceedings afterwards in his mind and "replay" the meeting. During the second thinking, he will provide the good comments he could have made in order to "star."

Some show of knowledge. Showing off knowledge and demonstrating expertness are somewhat different from communicating information or explaining technical matters. The person who is primarily interested in making a good impression may talk rapidly and introduce technical words. By this tactic he hopes to impress others with his knowledge without opening himself to embarrassing questions. Most professions have developed a tradition of protecting the expertness of their members from the layman by means of a complicated vocabulary. Technical terms can serve a useful function in naming clearly defined concepts. The expert may change his purpose from defending his status to explaining technical matters. When he does so, he may still use a technical vocabulary; the change in attitude, however, should result in a change in presentation. (An expert may have developed such strong habits of defending his status that even when he wants to communicate, he no longer has the requisite skills.) Generally, a person who wants to inform will introduce the technical concepts more slowly, will define them carefully, and will encourage questions and feedback.

Cohesiveness, the Key to Successful Communication

Cohesiveness and feedback. When a group achieves a stable role structure and a high level of cohesiveness, an increase in feedback usually follows. A person who is strongly attracted to the group and wishes it well will want to maximize communication. He knows that the group will do a better job if each member is thoroughly briefed. Therefore, if he does not know, he is more likely to ask. In addition, if he has a stable place in the group, admitting his ignorance does not hurt his reputation. Sometimes bad habits that developed during role struggles carry over and groups continue to function without adequate feedback. The group should make periodic evaluations of the feedback and make conscious plans to encourage it as needed.

Cohesiveness and listening. Just as the need to appear more knowledgeable disappears with stable structure, so does the need to show off. A person can relax and be honest in a group with a high level of cohesiveness. Again, the change in attitude should result in more concentration on listening to the message. When roles stabilize, the members do not feel the need any longer to view each message in personal terms. That is, they no longer bother with thinking: does this message mean so-and-so is leadership material? that he likes me? that he doesn't like me much? and so forth. Members can become "message centered," which is a first step to improved listening. The personnel in an organization will vary as to their skills in the arts of communication. Some may have trouble listening even with a proper attitude. Others may have difficulty expressing ideas; others may have trouble holding long chains of argument in mind. Achieving effective communication takes considerable time and tension-producing effort. Communication is hard work. Groups should establish the rule that enough time will be allocated and spent (not wasted) to assure that the proper level of understanding is reached during the meeting.

Cohesiveness and status. Formal status within a community or organization poses an almost insurmountable barrier to successful communication. The presence of a high status person in a meeting immediately inhibits the free flow of communication and feedback. People wait for the high status person to take the lead; they wait for cues from him as to the proper tone of response. They tend to tell the high status person only what they think he would like to hear. If a feeling of cohesiveness is generated within the work group, the problem of the high status person can be met to some extent. If the others discover that he is sincerely interested in the good of the group, that he tolerates disagreements, that he recognizes the necessity of sound communication, a productive meeting should follow.

Communicating Through Meetings

The uses of meetings. Meetings are essential to effective communication within the modern organization. The meeting provides a chance to inform members directly about important matters. The meeting is an excellent tool to build cohesiveness. It identifies the work group and gives it a chance to develop a tradition. The meeting can provide a channel for upward communication. Meetings and discussions are also techniques for solving problems and developing policy.

The abuses of meetings. Some meetings are held for no good reason. Perhaps originally the meeting may have served a function but, as time goes by, the organization changes and the meeting loses its purpose. The meeting is held out of habit. Meetings are also used as administrative dodges. One way for an administrator to handle a touchy issue is to "bury it" in committee. Finally, an administrator may use the meeting as a smoke screen for a decision. In such an instance, he has already made up his mind, but he pretends that the meeting will have an effect on the decision. After a time, the people in the meeting catch on to what is happening. They know that the meeting is simply a show, that the "old man" has already made up his mind, and that nothing said in the meeting will change things. Such meetings are time wasters.

Kinds of meetings. Work groups use several different sorts of meetings. If they come with the wrong expectation of what kind of meeting they are attending, they may find the meeting frustrating. For example, if the meeting is ceremonial and the person who came expected it to be used to make decisions, he would feel cheated.

(1) *The ritualistic meeting.* Every organization has some meetings that are rituals. In addition to aiding the cohesiveness of the

organization, these meetings assure that people of authority are recognized. For example, the department heads may make an oral presentation of their yearly budget to a meeting of all vice-presidents. The meeting puts a rubber stamp on decisions already made. Yet the meeting is important to the social interaction of the organization. The Young Turk who says this meeting accomplishes nothing and is therefore a waste of time is judging it on the wrong grounds.

(2) *The briefing meeting.* The briefing session is designed to provide members with the information to carry through on plans already laid. The objective is clear and people need only to find out who is to do what, when, and where.

(3) *The instructional meeting.* A meeting may be used to teach people in order to make them more proficient in their tasks.

(4) *The consultative meeting.* A consultative meeting is one wherein the person responsible for a decision asks the members for advice. He remains responsible for the decision, but he does ask and consider their advice.

(5) *The decision-making meeting.* One of the most difficult and yet most useful meetings is that designed to make decisions and formulate courses of action. *Members who help make, and who are responsible for, decisions are usually more fully committed to them and work harder to implement the action.*

Planning the Meeting

Be sure you need a meeting. Do not have a meeting unless it is absolutely necessary. Meetings are the heavy artillery of an organization's communications. A wise general uses his heavy artillery sparingly because it is expensive and difficult to maneuver. On the other hand, when he does need his big guns, he really has no satisfactory substitute for them. If the communication can be handled by individual conferences, telephone conversations, memorandums, or other techniques, the meeting is probably unnecessary.

Determine the purpose of the meeting. Every meeting should have a clear and specific purpose. Make sure the others know the purpose either before the meeting starts or very early in the session.

Plan the meeting to achieve the purpose. Where is the best place to hold the meeting? What format will best achieve the purpose? Should you use a slide lecture with questions and answers for a briefing session? Have brief reports from several members followed by questions and answers for a consultative meeting? A round table discussion of an agenda for policy-making? Also, who should take part in the meeting? Should people with special knowledge be invited? Should some high status people be invited to keep fences mended within the organization? Who might jeopardize the outcome if he felt hurt because he was not informed or consulted? Who should chair the meeting?

Plan the little details. A successful meeting requires time and effort in the planning stages. Don't neglect the planning. You may save time for your own work that way, but wasting the time of your colleagues in a useless meeting is not wise. Little things like providing pads and pencils, refreshments, properly arranged (and sufficient) seating – all these contribute to the success of the meeting. When minor details of administration are handled smoothly, the people get the feeling that the meeting is important and that it is going to do significant work.

Specify the outcomes of the meeting. This is not the same as deciding on the purposes. If plans are to be made, how will they be developed? In detail? In general outline? Decide what decisions can be made in such a meeting and in what form they should be made.

Utilize the results of the meeting. The substantive results of the meeting should be used. What can be done to follow up and apply the results of the conference? Do not let important leads drop at the end of the meeting.

Evaluate the meeting systematically. Spend some time evaluating the effectiveness of the meeting. We always make an informal evaluation of a meeting as we walk away from it. We may say to someone else, or just to ourselves, that it was a good meeting, or that we talked all around the subject, or that it was a waste of time. Some member of the group should collect impressions of the strengths and weaknesses of the meeting. These evaluations should be fed back to the participants. One of the striking discoveries in the study of groups is that they seldom spend any time talking about the *group* and about *how it functions.* Groups tend to concentrate on the job and ignore the important matters discussed in Parts I and II of this book. When groups do spend short periods after the meeting talking, as a group, about what happened in the meeting, about what was good and what was bad, the cohesiveness and effectiveness of the meetings are increased. Often things that are very disturbing when hidden from others evaporate when brought out into the open and discussed. Perhaps one person with some education in group process should be asked to serve as an evaluator of the meeting, and he can present a systematic statement to start the discussion.

Techniques for Leading the Meeting

Directing the meeting. Research indicates two situations in which people will willingly accept direction from the conference leader. The first is when he is the natural leader of the group. The second is when a group of relative strangers are meeting only once. Assuming a willingness to follow his direction, the leader will still need certain basic skills in order to conduct an efficient meeting. The three basic techniques for this purpose are: the question, the summary, and the directive. Summaries are always useful to indicate progress and to orient the group. The democratic style requires a higher proportion of questions to directives; the authoritarian style, more directives than questions.

(1) *Getting the meeting started.* The first problem is to get the group down to business. A certain amount of time should be devoted to releasing primary tension, but then the group must go to work. Questions are very useful. Open-ended questions are asked in such a way that they cannot be answered with a simple "yes" or "no." An open-ended question can get things started. The leader should set the mood for short and to-the-point comments early. If the first comment runs too long, the leader may have to interrupt with a question directed to someone else.

(2) *Keeping to the point.* An agenda, wisely used, will help the efficiency of a meeting. The agenda should not be too long. Too often, we are overly optimistic about what can be accomplished in a meeting of an hour or an hour-and-a-half. (It is unwise to run meetings much longer than two hours.) Keeping the agenda short assures adequate time for real communication. Do not expect the group to march through the steps of the agenda like a computer. Individuals, when

they are thinking hard, do not organize their thoughts in outline fashion, and groups must kick an idea around a little, too. Decisions emerge from work sessions much like roles emerge. Too often we judge a meeting as inefficient because the discussion wandered from the agenda. Sometimes the bypath is unnecessary and a waste of time, but some jumping from topic to topic is absolutely essential. This is the way decisions emerge in the work group. The members approach the entire problem several times to get the "lay of the land." Someone submits an idea. Others contribute facts, advice, opinions. A number of ideas are displayed. As they "kick" the ideas around, they sharpen their questions and discover areas of disagreement. They need to find the safe ground and the touchy points. They approach the entire problem at a superficial level, return again to dig more deeply, swing away and come back again to probe closer to the core, and finally make their decision. Of course, if the meeting is a briefing session or a meeting for instructional purposes, the topics on the agenda should be covered in order.

The leader needs to watch carefully, therefore, and make running choices about the drift of the discussion. Is it part of the necessary "kicking around of an idea?" Is it a waste of time? He should not take the easy way out and make the choice on the letter of the agenda. When he decides that it is a waste of time, he should bring the meeting back to the agenda. Questions are most useful for this: "Can we tie this in with the point about the language requirement?" "Just a minute; how does this relate to the liberal arts?" Summaries can give an overview of the last few minutes of the meeting and leave the group on the agenda. Finally, a leader may simply assert that they are off the track and direct that they get back. "We seem to be getting off the subject. Let's get back to Bill's point."

(3) *Moving the meeting along.* We have emphasized the importance of not pushing the group too fast. Now we remind the leader that devoting twenty minutes to material that is worth five will cause restlessness and frustration. The leader should watch for signs that a topic has been exhausted. If members begin to repeat themselves, fidget, pause for a lack of something to say, the leader should move to the next item.

The summary is the best way to do so. A summary rounds off the discussion of a point and leads naturally to a new one. It also gives the group a feeling of accomplishment.

(4) *Coming to a decision.* From time to time the group will need to make decisions. The leader can help if he steps in at those points and asks, "Are we in substantial agreement on this point?" If the question is important he may call for a vote.

Applying group process to difficult situations. Often some tension-producing behavior creates an awkward moment for the leader and the participants. If the awkward situation is related to a role struggle within a work group, or if it is a result of inept communication skills on the part of the members, the insights from Part I and Part II should be used to work a permanent cure. Bringing the problem out into the open and discussing it is a good way. What we offer here are hints as to how to handle awkward situations immediately when they crop up in a given meeting — the "aspirin" of group treatment.

IF A GROUP MEMBER CREATES A PROBLEM

Symptoms	Reasons	What to do
Member won't participate.	Excessive primary tension. Feels lack of acceptance and status.	Involve him in conversation. Find out about his personal interests. Listen with interest to what he says. Devote some time to him, outside the discussion. When he does take part, make a special note of it. "That is a good point, Joe. We haven't been hearing enough from you. We appreciate hearing your position."
		Use questions to draw him out. Ask a direct open-ended question so that only he can answer. Do not use a question than can be answered "yes" or "no," and, of course, do not ask a question that he might be unable to answer for lack of information.

Symptoms	Reasons	What to do
Member is joker, life of the party.	Feels tension, wants to relieve it. Enjoys spotlight and likes to get laughs.	Encourage him when tensions need release. Laugh, compliment his wit. Ignore him when it is time to go to work and tensions are eased. He will soon learn that his role is the productive release of tensions, not to waste time laughing it up when the group should be discussing.
Member monopolizes discussion.	(a) Is involved in a role struggle. Is trying to impress group to achieve high status or leadership.	(a) Encourage him if he is contending for role that will benefit the group the most. If not, interrupt him and move to another discussant. In general, encourage the group to take care of him.

OR

	(b) Is full of the subject and is sincerely eager to get to work.	(b) Don't embarrass him or be sarcastic. You will need him in this role later. Do not let him monopolize or give long speeches. Interrupt politely and throw the ball to another discussant with a question.
Member is argumentative, obstinate.	(a) Involved in role struggle.	(a) Keep your own temper. Understand he is not inherently obstinate but is so in the context of this discussion. Don't let the group get too tense and excited. Antagonism breeds further antagonism and secondary tension. Remember, group is partly responsible for his behavior. What can group do to change it?

OR

Symptoms	Reasons	What to do
(b) Has strong personal convictions on topic.		(b) Examine his position carefully. Find merit in it if possible. Do not close your mind to the ideas just because they are expressed in an opinionated way. The group must examine all sides. In an emergency tell him time is short and you will be glad to talk to him later. Talk to him privately before the next meeting. Explain that his view is important, the group will consider it, but he must not destroy group effectiveness.

IF THE GROUP CREATES A PROBLEM

Symptoms	Reasons	What to do
Group is tired, apathetic, dull.	Marked lack of interest, low response rate, tired, yawning, quiet, polite.	Primary tension	Small talk, joshing, kidding, humor. Make them smile, chuckle, laugh. Display as much enthusiasm and energy as you can. Do not give up if the first attempts to release the tension fail — keep pumping enthusiasm until it is caught. Explain subject vividly, ask lots of easy questions, play the devil's advocate.
Group is resistant, antagonistic, hostile.	Members intent on showing off, justifying their ideas, proving their worth. Members argue, come in conflict, show personal antagonism.	Secondary tensions caused by role and status struggles.	Analyze member ability. Assess the most useful role for each. Agree and support members who assume suitable roles. When secondary tensions become distracting, joke, use humor (not ridicule or satire), change the subject. Remind the group of its objectives. If necessary, face situation and bring role struggles into the open — talk about the social interactions.

Symptoms	Reasons	What to do
Group is enthusiastic, responsive, active.	Members stimulate one another to ideas, enthusiastic agreement, everyone interested and involved.	Stable role structure. High level of feedback. Members forget themselves in their interest in topic.	Give the group its head. Do not worry too much about sticking to the planned agenda. The chaff can be sifted out later. Right now exploit the group's creativity.
Group is lost, confused, wants to go to work.	Members ask directions. Complain that they have been wasting time. Feel that the discussion lacks organization. Members say they want to do something.	Group has begun its role structure. Wants to leave social matters and get down to work.	Now is time to suggest a way of working. Provide division of work, provide agendas and suggestions for systematic ways to go about discussion. (If you do this in shakedown cruise it will be rejected or resisted. If you provide structure now it will be welcomed.)

A Brief Review of Key Ideas from Part III

* The basic parts of a unit of communication are a source, a message, channels, and a receiver: S-M-C-R.

* Nonverbal communication refers to the information conveyed by the way a person talks and acts over and above (or in place of) the message conveyed by his words.

* Meanings, like motives, are in people, not in messages.

* Feedback refers to the questions, comments, facial expressions, and so forth that indicate how much the listener understands from a message.

* Cohesiveness encourages members of a work group to try to achieve communication rather than to show off or confuse.

* Meetings are the heavy artillery of organizational communication. Do not have a meeting unless it is necessary.

* Groups too seldom spend time talking about the group and the way it works. Systematic evaluations of meetings increase efficiency.

* People willingly accept leadership in a meeting if the moderator is the natural leader of a work group, or if the group is only meeting for one session.

* Decisions emerge from meetings in much the same way that roles emerge in work groups.

CHECKLIST 1 — Before the Meeting

Put this checklist in a handy place and use it to plan every meeting:

1. What is the purpose of the meeting? Ritual? Briefing? Instruction? Consultation? Decision-making?

2. What are the outcomes to emerge from the meeting?

3. What type of conference will best achieve the purpose? Lecture and discussion? Short presentation by several people to be followed by discussion? Open discussion? Parliamentary meeting?

4. Who will participate? Have we left out someone who should be invited? Included someone who need not be involved?

5. Who will serve as leader?

6. Where is the best place to hold the meeting? What is a good time? How long should the meeting last?

7. How and when will the participants be briefed on the meeting and given directions for preparation?

8. What physical details need to be taken care of? Will the room be ready and open? Ventilation or heating? Audiovisual aids? Can we guard against unnecessary distractions? Refreshments advisable?

9. How will the proceedings and results be recorded?

10. Who will prepare the agenda? Will it be circulated in advance?

11. How will the meeting be evaluated?

12. What will be done to "follow up" and apply the results of the meeting?

(Additional "checks" of your own?)

CHECKLIST 2 — After the Meeting

Summary checklist for evaluating a meeting. May be used by an individual in the group or by an observer who reports to the group:

1. Was the preparation for the meeting adequate? Equipment available when needed and in working order? Necessary information furnished to members? Rooms? Visual aid? Physical requirements met?

2. Was the purpose of the meeting clear to all? Were objectives of the meeting clearly specified? Did the leader introduce the agenda clearly and concisely?

3. Was a permissive social climate established? Primary tension released? Did all members participate?

4. Was the nonverbal communication in tune with the purposes of the meeting?

5. Did the meeting stay on the agenda? Did the group have enough freedom to really work? Did the leader exercise the right amount of control? Did the participants keep their contributions short and to the point?

6. Did the meeting come to sound conclusions? Did the leader help the group reach a consensus?

7. How well did the leader handle difficult situations? The talkative person? The quiet member? Conflicts?

8. Were plans made to follow up and tie together the loose ends? In another meeting? In private conferences? By memorandums?

9. What three things can be done to improve the next meeting?

CHECKLIST 3 – Your Own Leadership

If you were the leader for the meeting, here is a checklist to see how well you "led" the meeting; be honest with yourself; if you find a weak area, admit it and work to correct it for the next group meeting you must conduct:

1. Did you help dissipate primary tension? Were you friendly? Did you "loosen up" the group before plunging into the discussion?

2. Did you build group solidarity? Did your nonverbal as well as verbal communication indicate enthusiasm for the discussion and its importance?

3. Did you arrange the group so they could see and talk with one another? Did you invite latecomers to take a place that brough. them into the discussion?

4. Did you make an opening statement, informally, suggesting that everyone is expected to take part?

5. Did you pose a challenging question to start the discussion? One that required thinking, not guessing, more than yes or no?

6. Were you patient? Did you give the group time enough to get acquainted? Did you listen to and respect the opinions and viewpoints of others, especially those who disagreed with you?

7. Did you let the group identify the issues and procedures and then guide them along the path they selected?

8. Did you construct "on-the-spot" thought-provoking questions?

9. Did you listen for places when the group had finished a topic, and then did you summarize for the group?

10. Did you refer questions back to the group instead of trying to answer them all yourself?

11. Did you talk less than twenty per cent of the time?

12. Did you draw out the backward or reticent person?

13. Did you tactfully handle the problem of the talkative and opinionated discussants? Did you balance participation among the discussants and tactfully discourage irrelevant discussions?

Appendix

A Sequence of Student Projects for Experience in Small Group Communication

The following sequence of student projects moves from an in-depth group experience to public discussion to a careful evaluation of the dynamics of the group experience. An instructor can modify and expand or contract the sequence to fit a unit or a course that varies in length.

Project 1. Leaderless group discussion. The class is divided into groups of four, five, or six without an assigned leader, moderator, or chairman. Each group has a clear objective and a specific deadline in which it is to complete its work. Each group has, if possible, a tape recorder and a place to meet that provides some privacy. The group's task is to select an important topic relating to school, community, state, national, or world affairs, phrase a good discussion question, investigate the problem and, as a group, decide on the best solution.

Each group should have at least three and preferably four class periods to meet and work on their task. They may, of course, meet outside of class. The instructor may give the group one of several tasks. For example, he may require the group to write a task force report which contains their solution to the problem they have been investigating.

Project 2. Public discussion. The instructor may require the leaderless group discussions set up in Project 1 to prepare a public discussion for presentation to the class, or if there is not enough class time for each group to present a program before the class, the groups may prepare radio round table discussions to be entered into a competition, with the best of these to be played for the class.

Public discussion programs may allow for audience questions and comments, in which case they are called *forum* discussions. Public discussions have a chairman or moderator who introduces both the topic and the participants to the audience. The general rules for guiding a discussion developed in Part III of this book govern the chairman or moderator of the public discussion.

The opening part of the discussion program may be organized as a *symposium* discussion. In a symposium discussion the members divide the topic among themselves, and each member makes a brief comment about his subdivision of the topic after the program has been introduced by the moderator. The opening speeches are usually carefully prepared, timed, and uninterrupted. Following the round of opening comments, the discussion may become a forum with everyone participating, or the discussants may take a few minutes to question one another about the content of their speeches.

The opening part of the discussion program may be organized as a *panel* discussion. In the panel discussion the participants all take part in discussing each point on the program outline. The atmosphere of a panel is less formal than that of the symposium, and the members interrupt one another as they aim to create the illusion of spontaneity and the give-and-take of a typical work meeting of their task force. The main difference between the panel discussion program and a group work meeting is that the program is carefully planned as to agenda and the amount of time to be devoted to each portion of the outline. A good procedure is to devote about one-half of the class period to the panel discussion and then turn the meeting into a forum and allow questions and comments from the rest of the class.

A *radio round table* discussion is much like a panel. The students sit around the microphone and converse about the topic in a radio studio or in a classroom with a tape recorder, and the tape is later played for the rest of the class. Since voice identification is important in radio discussions, care must be taken with the way the participants are introduced so the listeners can clearly sort out the voices. Students may wish to use background music and develop a "format" which makes the program sound more professional.

Project 3. The evaluation of the leaderless group discussion. The students should keep a record of their experiences in the work group. They can do this by keeping a diary of each meeting which they prepare immediately afterwards and which answers such questions as: What happened to me in the last meeting? What happened to my group?

After the groups complete the leaderless group discussion assignment and the discussion programs, the class should conduct a brief postmortem and apply the concepts and principles of the book to their experiences. Ideally, the groups should meet again for several class days and make a case study of their own groups in which they examine how their experiences reflect and illustrate the material in Parts I and II of this book.

The following questions can profitably be discussed in such a group postmortem:

Did some members begin to specialize in certain tasks?
Did roles develop?
Did some members gain in status and influence?
What norms emerged in the group?
Who assumed the guidance functions for the group?
Was there contention over leadership?
Was the leadership question settled? If so, how?
How did the group process information?
How were opinions submitted and evaluated?
How were solutions given and tested?

The tape recordings of the meeting will be very helpful sources of information to aid the group in answering the above questions. The diaries that record the members' experiences will also help.

If class time is not available for group postmortems, each student may write a paper presenting an individual analysis of the dynamics of the group, including responses to some or all of the above questions. The importance of working in small groups within this framework of constant evaluation, during the actual work sessions and afterwards, brings most students more insight into the dynamic nature of small group communication than the mere learning of theory and principle can possibly provide.

Teaching Speech Communication Through Small Groups

The instructor of a speech communication class has many opportunities to use small group communication as a teaching method for instructing students in other forms of speech and communication. Groups can be used to teach a unit in public speaking by having students meet in small groups to study a problem, plan, and rehearse public speeches. After receiving the group's suggestions, criticisms, and help, the student speakers can revise their efforts before giving them to the larger audience of the entire class. Groups can also be used to work up readings for oral interpretation of literature, to plan play productions, and to produce radio and television shows.

If the instructor wishes, he can have the students read this book, discuss its concepts, and then use small group techniques to teach other units in the course. The students can keep a journal of their group experiences throughout the term and periodically spend a class meeting in postmortems of their group experiences, or students may also write reports evaluating their experiences and discussing the questions suggested in Project 3 above.

Sources

The best place to turn for additional information and a more complete and detailed analysis of small group communication along the lines laid down in this book is:

Bormann, Ernest G. *Discussion and Group Methods.* New York: Harper and Row, Publishers, 1969.

The sources referred to in the text are as follows:

Allport, Gordon W. *Pattern and Growth in Personality.* New York: Holt, Rinehart and Winston, Inc., 1961.

Bales, Robert F. *Interaction Process Analysis.* Cambridge: Addison-Wesley, 1950.
_____. *Personality and Interpersonal Behavior.* New York: Holt, Rinehart and Winston, Inc., 1970.
Berlo, David K. *The Process of Communication.* New York: Holt, Rinehart and Winston, Inc., 1960.
Hare, A. Paul. *Handbook of Small Group Research.* New York: The Free Press of Glencoe, 1962.
Howell, William S. Chapter 15, "Motive Analysis for the Persuader," in Bormann, Ernest G., William S. Howell, Ralph G. Nichols, and

George L. Shapiro. *Interpersonal Communication in the Modern Organization.* Englewood Cliffs, N. J.: Prentice-Hall, Inc., 1969.

Lickert, Rensis. *New Patterns of Management.* New York: McGraw-Hill Book Company, 1961.

McGregor, Douglas. *The Human Side of Enterprise.* New York: McGraw-Hill Book Company, 1960.

Maier, Norman R. F. *Problem-Solving Discussion and Conferences: Leadership Methods and Skills.* New York: McGraw-Hill Book Company, 1963.

Maslow, Abraham H. *Motivation and Personality.* New York: Harper and Row, Publishers, 1954.

Menninger, Karl. *Love Against Hate.* New York: Harcourt, Brace and World, Inc., 1942.

Index